LOIMOLOG

OR, AN
Historical Account
OF THE
Plague in *London* in 1665:

By
NATHANIEL HODGES
and JOHN QUINCY

THE
PREFACE.

IT may be needless to acquaint the Reader *why the following* Sheets *are published at this Time, we being all but too justly apprised of the Danger there may be, of wanting those Helps, which are here intended to be supplied, as far as such Means as these can do it.*

THE Treatise of Dr. Hodges *contains the best Account of the late Visitation by a* Plague *here in* England, *of any hitherto extant; and though some Readers may indeed observe, that the Enthusiastick Strain of the preceeding Times very much hurts his Style and Perspicuity; such an Influence had the Spirit of Delusion even over Matters of Science: However, the most affected Peculiarities and Luxuriancies of that kind are here avoided.*

WHAT is hereunto added, hath been partly extracted from Papers wrote some Years ago, and partly put together since our present Apprehensions from Abroad. The Enumeration of so many Causes of a Pestilence, or like Changes, as have no Relation to the present Case, may to some perhaps seem superfluous; but my Design hereby, was only the better to inculcate a right Understanding of a Contagion, *which is the last Consequence, and highest Degree of Aggravation they are capable of rising to; and gradually to lead Persons, not well accustomed to such Matters, from the more obvious, to the more secret Means of bringing such terrible Changes into our Constitutions.*

WHAT relates to such precautionary Means for our Security against the present Infection now Abroad, as concern the Magistrate, I have presumed to say but very little to; because I understand such Instructions are now waited for from a very great and able Physician: But, with Submission to the wisest, I cannot but repeat it here again, that no humane Means seems more absolutely necessary, than to remove the Infected immediately upon their Seizure, out of all great Towns, and provide for their due Support in all Things, in open Country Places; for the Distemper becomes not infectious till some Time after Seizure.

AS for what every Person may do for his private Safety, I have given several additional Hints, either fuller or plainer than Dr. Hodges *hath done. And because his Antidotes and precautionary Medicines are now obsolete, and not by much so elegant or easie to be procured, as the present Practice and Shops do supply, I have added some* Formulæ, *to be complied with, or altered, as different Exigencies, and better Judges may think fit.*

IF the Reader should be curious enough to note any Incorrectnesses of Style, or Typographical Errors, he is desired to excuse them, from the great Hurry which these Sheets passed through the Press in, although there hath been as much Care taken to prevent either, as so much Hast with which they were called for would admit of.

LOIMOLOGIA:

OR, AN

ACCOUNT, *&c.*
SECTION I.

Of the Rise and Progress of the late
PLAGUE.

THE Plague which we are now to give an Account of, discovered the Beginnings of its future Cruelties, about the Close of the Year 1664; for at that Season two or three Persons died suddenly in one Family at *Westminster*, attended with like Symptoms, that manifestly declared their Origin: Hereupon some timorous Neighbours, under Apprehensions of a Contagion, removed into the City of *London*, who unfortunately carried along with them the pestilential Taint; whereby that Disease, which was before in its Infancy, in a Family or two, suddenly got Strength, and spread Abroad its fatal Poisons; and meerly for Want of confining the Persons first seized with it, the whole City was in a little Time irrecoverably infected. Not unlike what happened the Year following, when a small Spark, from an unknown Cause, for Want of timely Care, increased to such a Flame, that neither the Tears of the People, nor the Profusion of their *Thames*, could extinguish; and which laid Wast the greatest Part of the City in three Days Time: And therefore as there happens to be no great Difference between these two grievous Calamities, this Mention of them together may not be improper; and the more especially, because by a like irresistable Fate from a Fever and a Conflagration, both the Inhabitants and their Houses were reduc'd to Ashes.

BUT as soon as it was rumoured amongst the common People, who are always enough astonished at any Thing new, that the Plague was in the City, it is impossible to relate what Accounts were spread of its Fatality, and well were it, had not the Presages been so ominous; every one predicted its future Devastations, and they terrified each other with Remembrances of a former Pestilence; for it was a received Notion amongst the common People, that the Plague visited *England* once in Twenty Years; as if after a certain Interval, by some inevitable Necessity, it must return again. But although this Conceit, how well soever justify'd by past Experiences, did not so much obtain with Persons of more Judgment, yet this may be affirmed, that it greatly contributed, amongst the Populace, both to propagate and inflame the Contagion, by the strong Impressions it made upon their Minds.

AND these frightful Apprehensions were not a little increased by the Predictions of Astrologers, from the Conjunctions of Stars, and the Appearances of Comets;[4] for although but little Regard was given to such Things by Persons of Thought, yet Experience daily shewed, what Influence they had with the meaner Sort, whose Spirits being manifestly sunk by such Fears, rendered their Constitutions less able to resist the Contagion. Whosoever duly considers it, can never imagine that this Pestilence had its Origin from any Conjunction of *Saturn* and *Jupiter*, in *Sagitarius* on the Tenth of *October*, or from a Conjunction of *Saturn* and *Mars* in the same Sign on the Twelfth of *November*, which was the common Opinion; for all the Good that happens during the like Conjunctions is assignable to the same Causes.

THE like Judgment is to be made of Comets, how terrible soever they may be in their Aspects, and whether they are produced in the higher Regions from a Conglomeration of many Stars, and returning at certain Periods; or whether they are lower, and the Production of sulphureous Exhalations, kindled in our own Atmosphere; For there is nothing strange in the Accension of heterogeneous Particles into a Flame, upon their rapid Occursions and Collisions against each other, howsoever[5] terrible the Tracks of such Light may be circumstanced. The People therefore were frightned without Reason at such Things, and the Mischief was much more in the Predictions of the Star-Gazers, than in the Stars themselves: Nothing could however conquer these sad Impressions, so powerful were they amongst the Populace, who anticipated their unhappy Fate with their Fears, and precipitated their own Destruction.

BUT to pass by Things of less Moment, it is to be taken Notice, that a very hard Frost set in on *December*, which continued three Months, and seemed greatly to deaden the Contagion, and very few died during that Season; although even then it was not extinguished, for in the Middle of *Christmas* Holy-days, I was called to a Young-Man in a Fever, who after two Days Course of alexiterial Medicines, had two Risings about the Bigness of a Nutmeg broke out, one on each Thigh; upon Examination of which, I soon discovered the Malignity, both from their black Hue, and the Circle round them, and pronounced it to be the Plague; in which Opinion I was afterwards confirmed[6] by subsequent Symptoms, although by God's Blessing the Patient recovered.

THIS Case I insert, both to shew that this Season did not wholly destroy the Distemper, although it greatly restrained it; but upon the Frost breaking, the Contagion got Ground, and gradually got out of its Confinements; like a Flame that for some Time seems smother'd, and suddenly breaks out with aggravated Fury.

AS soon as the Magistracy, to whom belonged the publick Care, saw how the Contagion daily increased, and had now extended it self to several Parishes, an Order was immediately issued out to shut up all the infected Houses, that neither Relations nor Acquaintance might unwarily receive it from them, and to keep the infected from carrying it about with them.

BUT whether this Method proved of Service or not, is to this Day doubtful, and much disputed; but it is my Business here however to adhere to Facts, and relate the Arguments on both Sides with all possible Impartiality.

7

IN Order whereunto, it is to be observ'd, that a Law was made for marking the Houses of infected Persons with a Red Cross, having with it this Subscription, *LORD HAVE MERCY UPON US*: And that a Guard should there continually attend, both to hand to the Sick the Necessaries of Food and Medicine, and to restrain them from coming Abroad until Forty Days after their Recovery. But although the *Lord Mayor* and all inferior Officers readily and effectually put these Orders in Execution, yet it was to no Purpose, for the Plague more and more increased; and the Consternation of those who were thus separated from all Society, unless with the infected, was inexpressible; and the dismal Apprehensions it laid them under, made them but an easier Prey to the devouring Enemy. And this Seclusion was on this Account much the more intolerable, that if a fresh Person was seized in the same House but a Day before another had finished the Quarantine, it was to be performed over again; which occasion'd such tedious Confinements of sick and well together, that sometimes caused the Loss of the whole.

8

BUT what greatly contributed to the Loss of People thus shut up, was the wicked Practices of Nurses (for they are not to be mention'd but in the most bitter Terms): These Wretches, out of Greediness to plunder the Dead, would strangle their Patients, and charge it to the Distemper in their Throats; others would secretly convey the pestilential Taint from Sores of the infected to those who were well; and nothing indeed deterred these abandoned Miscreants from prosecuting their avaritious Purposes by all the Methods their Wickedness could invent; who, although they were without Witnesses to accuse them, yet it is not doubted but divine Vengeance will overtake such wicked Barbarities with due Punishment: Nay, some were remarkably struck from Heaven in the Perpetration of their Crimes, and one particularly amongst many, as she was leaving the House of a Family, all dead, loaded with her Robberies, fell down dead under her Burden in the Streets: And the Case of a worthy Citizen was very remarkable, who being suspected dying by his Nurse, was before-hand stripped by her; but recovering again, he came a second 9 Time into the World naked. And so many were the Artifices of these barbarous Wretches, that it is to be hoped, Posterity will take Warning how they trust them again in like Cases; and that their past Impunities will not be a Means of bringing on us again the like Judgment.

MOREOVER, this shutting up infected Houses, made the Neighbours fly from theirs, who otherwise might have been a Help to them on many Accounts; and I verily believe that many who were lost might have now been alive, had not the tragical Mark upon their Door drove proper Assistances from them.

AND this is confirmed by the Examples of other pestilential Contagions, which have been observed not to cease, until the Doors of the Sick were let open, and they had the Privilege of going Abroad; of the same Authority is the Custom of other Nations, who have due Regard to that Liberty that is necessary for the Comforts both of Body and Mind.

IT now remains that we take Notice of all that is of any Weight on the other 10 Side; as therefore it is not at all deemed cruel to take off a mortify'd Limb to save the whole, by a Parity of Reason is the Conduct of a Community justifyable, who, out of a Regard to the Publick Good, put Hardships upon particular Persons; in a pestilential Contagion therefore, what can be of more immediate Service than securing those that are well from the Infection? And the more especially in a Disease that reaches not only the Body, but taints the very Breath; for in this Case the infected Breath poisons upon the healthful, and even at the Point of Death endeavours to diffuse that Venom to others that conquer'd them. From this delirious Pleasure arises those Tricks of transplanting the Corruption of a pestilential Tumour to another; not to say any Thing of that Woman, who with her Importunities drew her unhappy Husband into her Embraces, which ended his Life with hers.

AGAIN, to take away all Doubtings in this Case, I am not ignorant of what Moment it is, to shut up the Houses of all those who are infected, according to Custom; for by this means a Contagion may at first be stifled, which otherwise would go beyond 11 any Remedy; and with equal Advantage might Gun-Powder be fired, if too much Time is not wasted in Deliberation, before these Things are put into Practice.

BUT if hereafter again a Plague should break out, (which God forbid) with Submission to Superiors, I should think it not improper to appoint proper Accommodations out of the City, for such as are yet untouched in infected Families; and who should continue there for a certain Time; the Sick in the mean time to be removed to convenient Apartments provided on Purpose for them: For by this Means, that Practice so abhorrent to Religion and Humanity, even in the Opinion of a *Mahometan*, of shutting up the sick and well together, would be avoided.

BUT to return: The Infection had long doubtfully reign'd, and continued through *May* and *June*, with more or less Severity; sometimes raging in one Part, and then in another, as in a running sort of Fight; as often as the Number of Funerals decreased, great Hopes were conceived of its Disappearance; then on a sudden again their Increase threw all into Dejection, as if the whole City[12] was soon to be unpeopled; which Uncertainty gave Advantage to the Distemper; because Persons were more remiss in their Provisions against it, during such Fluctuation.

IT must not however be omitted, with what Precipitation the trembling Inhabitants left the City, and how they flocked in such Crowds out of Town, as if *London* had quite gone out of it self, like the Hurry of a sudden Conflagration, all Doors and Passages are thronged for Escape: Yet after the chief of the People were fled, and thereby the Nourishment of this cruel Enemy had been in a great Measure taken away, yet it raged still; and although it seemed once to slay as *Parthians* in their Flight, it soon returned with redoubled Fury, and kill'd not by slow Paces, but almost immediately upon Seizure; not unlike what is often seen in Battle, when after some Skirmishes of Wings, and separate Parties, the main Bodies come to engage; so did this Contagion at first only scatter about its Arrows, but at last covered the whole City with Death.

[13]

THUS therefore in the Space of one Week were eighty Persons cut off, and when Things came to Extremity, all Helps were called in; so it began now to be solely the Magistrates Business, how to put a Stop to this cruel Devastation, and save some Part of the City at last from the Grave; first then therefore were appointed a Monthly Fast for Publick Prayers, to deprecate the Anger of Heaven; nor proved it in vain, or were their Supplications altogether fruitless; for if we have any Regard to the Temperature of the Season, the whole Summer was refreshed with moderate Breezes, sufficient to prevent the Air's Stagnation and Corruption, and to carry off the pestilential Steams; the Heat was likewise too mild to encourage such Corruption and Fermentation, as helps to taint the animal Fluids, and pervert them from their natural State.

THE Government however, to the Duty of Publick Prayers, neglected not to add what Assistances might be had from Medicine; to which Purpose his Majesty, with the divine Helps, called in also all that was humane; and by his Royal Authority commanded the College of Physicians of *London*, jointly to write somewhat in *English* that might be a general Directory in this[14] calamitous Exigence: Nor was it satisfactory to that honoured Society to discharge their Regards for the Publick with that only, but some were chose out of their Number, and appointed particularly to attend the infected on all Occasions; two also out of the Court of Aldermen were required to see this hazardous Task executed; so that encouraged with all proper Means, this Province was chearfully undertaken, and all possible Caution was used fully to answer the Intention; but this Task was too much for four Persons, and wanted rather the Concurrence of the whole Faculty; we were however ashamed to give it up, and used our utmost Application therein; but all our Care and Pains were eluded, for the Disease, like the *Hydra's* Heads, was no sooner extinguished in one Family, but it broke out in many more with Aggravations; so that in a little Time we found our Task too great, and despaired of putting an entire Stop to the Infection.

NOR was there at this Time wanting the Help of very great and worthy Persons, who voluntarily contributed their Assistances in this dangerous Work; amongst the Number of which, the learned[15] Dr.*Glisson*, *Regius* Professor at *Cambridge*, Dr. *Nath. Paget*, Dr. *Wharton*, Dr. *Berwick*, Dr. *Brookes*, and many others who are yet alive, deserve very honourable Mention; but eight or nine fell in this Work, who were too much loaded with the

Spoils of the Enemy; and amongst whom was Dr. *Conyers*, whose Goodness and Humanity claim an honourable Remembrance with all who survive him.

AFTER then all Endeavours to restrain the Contagion proved of no Effect, we applied our selves altogether to the Care of the diseased; and in the Prosecution of which, it may be affirmed without Boasting, no Hazards to our selves were avoided: But it is incredible to think how the Plague raged amongst the common People, insomuch that it came by some to be called the *Poors Plague*; yet although the more opulent had left the Town, and that it was almost left uninhabited, the Commonalty that were left felt little of Want; for their Necessities were relieved with a Profusion of good Things from the Wealthy, and their Poverty was supported with Plenty; a more manifest Cause therefore for such a Devastation amongst them I shall assign in another Place.

IN the Months of *August* and *September*, the Contagion chang'd its former slow and languid Pace, and having as it were got Master of all, made a most terrible Slaughter, so that three, four, or five Thousand died in a Week, and once eight Thousand; who can express the Calamities of such Times? The whole *British* Nation wept for the Miseries of her Metropolis. In some Houses Carcases lay waiting for Burial, and in others, Persons in their last Agonies; in one Room might be heard dying Groans, in another the Ravings of a Delirium, and not far off Relations and Friends bewailing both their Loss, and the dismal Prospect of their own sudden Departure: Death was the sure Midwife to all Children, and Infants passed immediately from the Womb to the Grave; who would not burst with Grief, to see the Stock for a future Generation hang upon the Breasts of a dead Mother? Or the Marriage-Bed changed the first Night into a Sepulchre, and the unhappy Pair meet with Death in their first Embraces? Some of the infected run about staggering like drunken Men, and fall and expire in the Streets; while others lie half-dead and comatous, but[17] never to be waked but by the last Trumpet, some lie vomiting as if they had drunk Poison; and others fall dead in the Market, while they are buying Necessaries for the Support of Life. Not much unlike was it in the following Conflagration; where the Altars themselves became so many Victims, and the finest Churches in the whole World carried up to Heaven Supplications in Flames, while their Marble Pillars wet with Tears melted like Wax; nor were Monuments secure from the inexorable Flames, where many of their venerable Remains passed a second Martyrdom; the most august Palaces were soon laid Waste, and the Flames seemed to be in a fatal Engagement to destroy the great Ornament of Commerce; and the Burning of all the Commodities of the World together, seemed a proper Epitome of this Conflagration; neither confederate Crowns, nor the drawn Swords of Kings, could restrain its Phanatick and Rebellious Rage; large Halls, stately Houses, and the Sheds of the Poor, were together reduced to Ashes; the Sun blush'd to see himself set, and envied those Flames the Government of the Night, which had rivalled him so many Days;[18] as the City, I say, was afterwards burnt without any Distinction, in like Manner did this Plague spare no Order, Age, or Sex; The Divine was taken in the very Exercise of his priestly Office, to be inrolled amongst the Saints Above; and some Physicians, as before intimated, could not find Assistance in their own Antidotes, but died in the Administration of them to others; and although the Soldiery retreated from the Field of Death, and encamped out of the City, the Contagion followed, and vanquish'd them; many in their old Age, others in their Prime, sunk under its Cruelties; of the Female Sex most died; and hardly any Children escaped; and it was not uncommon to see an Inheritance pass successively to three or four Heirs in as many Days; the Number of Sextons were not sufficient to bury the Dead; the Bells seemed hoarse with continual tolling, until at last they quite ceased; the burying Places would not hold the Dead, but they were thrown into large Pits dug in waste Grounds, in Heaps, thirty or forty together; and it often happened that those who attended the Funerals of their Friends one Evening, were carried the next to their own long Home:

———— *Quis talia fundo Temperet à Lachrymis?* ————

Even the Relation of this Calamity melts me into Tears, and yet the worst was not certain, although the City was near drained by her Funerals; for the Disease as yet had no Relaxation.

ABOUT the Beginning of *September*, the Disease was at the Height; in the Course of which Month more than twelve Thousand died in a Week: But at length, that nothing might go untried to divert the Contagion, it was ordered by the Governours who were left to superintend those calamitous Affairs, (for the Court was then removed to *Oxford*) to burn Fires in the Streets for three Days together; yet while this was in Debate, the Physicians concerned were diffident of the Success, as the Air in it self was un-infected; and therefore rendred such a showy and expensive a Project superfluous, and of no Effect; and these Conjectures we supported by the Authority of Antiquity, and *Hippocrates* himself; notwithstanding which, the Fires were kindled in [20] all the Streets. But alas! the Controversie was soon decided; for before the three Days were quite expired, the Heavens both mourned so many Funerals, and wept for the fatal Mistake, so as to extinguish even the Fires with their Showers. I shall not determine any other Person's Conjecture in this Case, whether these Fires may more properly be deemed the ominous Forerunners of the ensuing Conflagration, or the ensuing Funerals; but whether it was from the suffocating Qualities of the Fuel, or the wet Constitution of Air that immediately followed, the most fatal Night ensued, wherein more than four Thousand expired. May Posterity by this Mistake be warned, and not, like Empyricks, apply a Remedy where they are ignorant of the Cause.

THE Reader is by the Way to be advertised, that this Year was luxuriant in most Fruits, especially Cherries and Grapes, which were at so low a Price, that the common People surfeited with them; for this might very much contribute to that Disposition of Body as made the pestilential Taint more easily take Place.

[21]

NOR ought we here to pass by the beneficent Assistances of the Rich, and the Care of the Magistrates; for the Markets being open as usual, and a greater Plenty of all Provisions, was a great Help to support the Sick; so that there was the Reverse of a Famine, which hath been observed to be so fatal to pestilential Contagions; and in this the Goodness of Heaven is always to be remembred, in alleviating a common Misery by such a Profusion of good Things from the Stores of Nature.

BUT as it were to balance this immediate Help of Providence, nothing was otherwise wanting to aggravate the common Destruction; and to which nothing more contributed than the Practice of Chymists and Quacks, and of whose Audacity and Ignorance it is impossible to be altogether silent; they were indefatigable in spreading their Antidotes; and although equal Strangers to all Learning as well as Physick, they thrust into every Hand some Trash or other under the Disguise of a pompous Title. No Country sure ever abounded with such [22] wicked Impostors; for all Events contradicted their Pretensions, and hardly a Person escaped that trusted to their Delusions: Their Medicines were more fatal than the Plague, and added to the Numbers of the Dead: But these Blowers of the pestilential Flames were caught in the common Ruin, and by their Death in some Measure excused the Neglect of the Magistracy, in suffering their Practice:

——— *Nec Lex est justior ulla Quàm necis Artifices Arte perire suâ.*

ABOUT this Time a Person of Distinction and great Humanity, going to *France* upon some Affairs of State, heard that some *Frenchmen* were Masters of an Antipestilential Remedy, and took Care to send some Doses of it over here: By Command of the Government we were ordered to try it with due Caution, which we did with Expectations of uncommon Success, but *the Mountain brought forth Death*; for the Medicine, which was a Mineral Preparation, threw the Patients into their last Sleep. May it never hereafter be injoined to try Experiments with unknown and foreign Medicines, upon the Lives even [23] of the meanest Persons! For certainly nothing is more abhorrent to Reason, than to impose a universal Remedy, in Cases whose curative Intentions are different, and sometimes opposite; and the various Indications of a Pestilence require very different Methods of Remedy, as shall hereafter be further demonstrated.

TO this may be added, that many common Medicines were publickly Sold, which by their extraordinary Heat and Disposition to inflame the Blood, could never be fit for every Age, Sex, and Constitution indifferently, and therefore in many Cases must undoubtedly do Harm. On this Account not only the *Sacred Art*, but the *Publick Health* also suffered; yet we who were particularly employed in this Affair as Physicians, used all Sollicitations with the

Magistracy to restrain such Practices, in Order to stop the Ruin they aggravated. Hence notwithstanding it was made a Question, whether in a Plague, where so many Physicians retire, (not so much for their own Preservation, as the Service of those whom they attend) it is not expedient for every one, according to his Abilities, to do his utmost[24] in averting the common Ruin? In the same Manner as in a Fire all Hands are required, even of the Croud as well as Workmen, to extinguish it.

B U T in this Case my own Opinion is determined: In the Restauration of Health, a Person must proceed with more Caution and Deliberation than in the supposed Case of a Fire; for there are Difficulties occur in the Practice of Medicine which are insuperable but by the unlearned; and the fine Texture of a humane Body is not to be managed by as clumsie Hands as the Materials of a House; in the former, if a Person makes a Mistake, it is with great Difficulty repaired; and therefore upon a serious Consideration of the whole Affair, I cannot make any Doubt, but that it is much better even to want Physicians in such Calamities, than to have the Sick under the Care and Management of the unlearned; for such Persons, like those who fight blindfold, know not in what Parts to attack the Enemy, nor with what Weapons to do it; besides which, they also are in Hazard of obstructing these Efforts of Nature, which would many Times, without Help, if not thus hindred, get the better of the Distemper.

[25]

NOR in this Account are we to neglect, that the Contagion spread its Cruelties into the neighbouring Countries; for the Citizens, which crowded in Multitudes into the adjacent Towns, carried the Infection along with them, where it raged with equal Fury; so that the Plague, which at first crept from one Street to another, now reigned over whole Counties, leaving hardly any Place free from its Insults; and the Towns upon the *Thames* were more severely handled, not perhaps from a great Moisture in the Air from thence, but from the tainted Goods rather that were carried upon it: Moreover, some Cities and Towns, of the most advantageous Situation for a wholsome Air, did notwithstanding feel the common Ruine. Such was the Rise, and such the Progress, of this cruel Destroyer, which first began at *London*.

B U T the worst Part of the Year being now over, and the Height of the Disease, the Plague by leisurely Degrees declined, as it had gradually made its first Advances; and before the Number infected decreased, its Malignity began to relax, insomuch that few died, and those chiefly such as[26] were ill managed; hereupon that Dread which had been upon the Minds of the People wore off; and the Sick chearfully used all the Means directed for their Recovery; and even the Nurses grew either more cautious, or more faithful; insomuch that after some Time a Dawn of Health appeared, as sudden, and as unexpected, as the Cessation of the following Conflagration; wherein after blowing up of Houses, and using all Means for its Extinction to little Purpose, the Flames stopped as it were of themselves, for Want of Fuel, or out of Shame for having devoured so much.

THE Pestilence did not however stop for Want of Subjects to act upon, (as then commonly rumoured) but from the Nature of the Distemper, its Decrease was like its Beginning, moderate; nor is it less to be wondred at, that as at the Rise of the Contagion all other Distempers went into that, so now at its Declension that degenerated into others, as *Inflammations, Head-achs, Quinseys, Dysenteries, Small-Pox, Measles, Fevers,* and *Hecticks*; wherein that also yet predominated, as hereafter will be further shewn.

[27]

A B O U T the Close of the Year, that is, on the Beginning of *November*, People grew more healthful, and such a different Face was put upon the Publick, that although the Funerals were yet frequent, yet many who had made most Hast in retiring, made the most to return, and came into the City without Fear; insomuch that in *December* they crowded back as thick as they fled: The Houses which before were full of the Dead, were now again inhabited by the Living; and the Shops which had been most Part of the Year shut up, were again opened, and the People again chearfully went about their wonted Affairs of Trade and Employ; and even what is almost beyond Belief, those Citizens, who before were afraid even of their Friends and Relations, would without Fear venture into the Houses and Rooms where infected Persons had but a little before breathed their Last: Nay, such Comforts did inspire the languishing People, and such Confidence, that many went into the Beds where Persons had died before they were even cold, or cleansed from the Stench of the Diseased; they had the Courage now to marry again, and betake to the Means of repairing the past Mortality; and even Women before deemed barren, were said to prove proliffick; so that although the Contagion had carried off, as some computed, about one hundred thousand, after a few Months their Loss was hardly discernable, and thus ended this fatal Year.

BUT the next Spring indeed appeared some Remains of the Contagion, which was easily conquered by the Physicians, and like the Termination of a common *Intermittent*, ended in a healthful Recovery: Whereupon the whole Malignity ceasing, the City returned to a perfect Health; not unlike what happened also after the last Conflagration, when a new City suddenly arose out of the Ashes of the old, much better able to stand the like Flames another Time.

SECTION II.

Of the Cause of a Pestilence, and a Contagion.

AS it is our Purpose here to enquire into the Origin of the late Plague, and find out both its manifest and hidden Causes; I cannot judge it necessary to go into the usual Length of Writers, in a particular Recital of all those remote Regards which they distinguish by Supernatural, Preternatural, and Natural; because by such Means this Treatise would be drawn out into an almost infinite needless Distinction.

THAT the Truth therefore may at once be brought into an open Light, and the Pestilence appear in its genuine Affections, I think it proper to premise this one Thing, because the whole depends upon it, *viz*. That the Pestilence is the most notorious of all popular Diseases, and depends upon some Cause equally common, and in every respect adequate to its extensive Effects; which being granted, it naturally follows, that all particular Causes which may accidentally intervene, (the Recital of which would be very tedious) are resolvable into this one.

AND for what concerns that Pestilence now under Enquiry, this we have as to its Origin, from the most irrefragable Authority, that it first came into this Island by Contagion, and was imported to us from *Holland*, in Packs of Merchandice; and if any one pleases to trace it further, he may be satisfied by common Fame, it came thither from *Turkey* in Bails of Cotton or Silk, which is a strange Preserver of the pestilential Steams. For that Part of the World is seldom free from such Infections, altho' it is sometimes more severe than others, according to the Disposition of Seasons and Temperature of Air in those Regions: But if any would yet more intimately be acquainted with its Origin, it concerns him to know all the Changes the Air in these Climates is subject to, and its various Properties of Dryness, Moisture, Heat, Cold, &c.

BUT least I should be thought too prolix in the Enumeration of such Circumstances, and incur the Suspicion of Atheism, (a Charge too just upon the Faculty) by ascribing too much to second Causes, as the Schools please to call them, it may be convenient for me to declare, that the το θειον of a Pestilence is as much a Part of my Faith, as any others; the sacred Pages clearly and demonstratively prove, that the Almighty, by his Authority, and at his Pleasure, may draw the Sword, bend the Bow, or shoot the Arrows of Death; and a Retrospection into Times past, shews many convincing Proofs of this terrible Truth; and in this Contagion before us, the Footsteps of an over-ruling Power are very legible, especially so far as concerns his divine Permission: But the great God's Purposes are Secrets too awful for Mortals to pry into, although we know that he punishes as a Parent, and chides for our Good, which makes it our Duty to kiss the Rod, and submit. But enough of this, least I should be thought to invade anothers Province; and it is sufficient to the Purpose of a Physician, to assign natural and obvious Causes; and where such are discoverable, it is unworthy of him and the divine Art he professes, as well as an Affront to good Sense, to have Recourse to any other.

32

BUT this being premised only to prevent Censure, our Way now lies open to a Discovery of the Nature of this Pestilence. Wherein, for Method Sake, I shall begin with a Description of a Pestilence in general; and which if it doth not exactly agree with the Accounts given by the Ancients, yet I doubt not but it will be found by every impartial Considerer, to be as full and satisfactory.

THE Pestilence is a Disease arising from an *Aura* that is poisonous, very subtle, deadly, and contagious, affecting many Persons at the same Time together in one Country, chiefly arising from a Corruption of the nitrous Spirit in the Air, attended with a Fever, and other very grievous Symptoms.

EVERY one of these Particulars are as clear as the Light at Noon-day; and these Explications are so obvious to be met with in the Writings of the Learned, that it would be lost Labour to insist upon any such Thing here; we shall therefore proceed to explain only what more immediately stands in need of it.

AND first of all it is said from an *Aura*, as distinguishing it from such Poison[33] as is more gross and earthy; for this is not to be confined in any Inclosure, but is so rare, subtle, volatile, and fine, that it insinuates into, and resides in the very Interstices, or Pores of the aerial Particles; whereas that which is of a more fixed Nature, is confined within certain Limits, and is incapable of such Progress.

IT is said to be poisonous also, from its Similitude to the Nature of a Poison, and both being equally destructive to Life, and killing Persons much after the same Manner, so that they seem to differ in Degree only; for the deadly Quality of a Pestilence vastly exceeds either the arsenical Minerals, the most poisonous Animals or Insects, or the killing Vegetables; nay, the Pestilence seems to be a Composition of all the other Poisons together, as well as in its fatal Efficacies to excel them, for in this there is manifestly joined both the Height of Putrefaction and Malignity. And as in a great man the Virulence of this Taint hath been discoverable, so in one Youth for Instance it was so remarkable, that even in the Point of Death the whole Body changed green, which so alarmed the Mother, that she immediately hasted[34] to my House, to know whether by Mistake there had not been some Poison given him; whereas he had taken nothing but mild and common Alexipharmicks; this green Hue therefore was a Demonstration of the poisonous Vitriolick Nature of the pestilential Taint.

IT is said to be very subtile both on Account of its Original and Production, before it hath escaped from its native Seat; and that wonderful Comminution which it cannot but undergo in its Progress through so many Climates, whereby it is, as it were, sublimed to the highest Degree of Volatility, beyond that of any Meteor, which is the Production of gross, corporeal, and heterogeneous Particles; nay, it is more active than Lightning, and in the Twinkling of an Eye carries to a Distance Putrefaction, Mortification, and Death.

AS for the Manner whereby it kills, its approaches are generally so secret, that Persons seized with it seem to be fallen into an Ambuscade, or a Snare, of which there was no Manner of Suspicion; they are therefore not to be credited or regarded, who affirm the Progress of a Pestilence to be sensible,[35] even to the Smell and Sight, and report (though who will may believe them for me) the Infection to resemble the Fragrancy of Flowers in *May*, or any other sweet Savour; or, on the contrary, to strike the Nose like the Stench of a rotten Carcase; nay, some pretend to be so sharp-sighted, as to discern Clouds in the Atmosphere big with pestilential Poysons, and other such Conceits of a distempered Imagination, that are chiefly the Products of Fear, which construes every Thing for the worst: Although indeed I must confess, that sometimes this very subtile *Aura* may be so mixed or loaded with gross and sulphureous Particles, as to be perceptible to the Senses.

FURTHER, as to the fatal Influences of a Plague, if the before recited Account is not sufficient to shew it, it would not be a Task of any Difficulty to produce many Instances of its Tyranny and Destruction: Hence the Plague by the *Hebrews* was called לבד, or Perdition; as if it was ordained on Purpose to destroy Mankind: It is also called *Lues*, from λυω, to dissolve, a most certain Way of Destruction, and whose fatal Property in the Plague is most remarkable, whereby it does not so much[36] prepare the Way, as immediately of its self destroy, and of whose certain Ruin, through whole Regions together, we have too many Testimonies upon Record, in the Writings both of Ancients and Moderns.

AGAIN, the Pestilence is said to be contagious; because some are come to that Height of Boldness, (being blind with too much Light) to propagate strange Conjectures to the contrary, as if the late Plague was begun and continued by a foreign Influence; but to remove this Controversie, it may be convenient to explain the Nature of a Contagion, and its supposed Conditions of Exertion; but before I enter upon this, it will be necessary to dispatch the other Members of this Definition.

IT is further added, that the Plague affects many Regions together at the same Time, in Order to distinguish it both from *Endemick* Diseases, that is, such as are appropriate to one Place only; and also from *Sporadick* Diseases, which although they rage amongst the Populace in this or that Country or Climate indifferently, according to the Influence of their procatarctick Causes, they are yet to be deemed particular, as[37] well as they are pernicious: But enough of these Matters.

AT length then it becomes necessary to change the Consideration, and enquire how it comes that the Plague hath its chief Origin from a Change or Corruption of the nitrous Spirits in the Air. This is the great Difficulty! This is our Task! It is therefore to be hoped that the Novelty of the Opinion will not occasion any one to receive it at first Sight amiss, until by due Examination he hath brought it to Trial; but in Order to erect this upon a sure Foundation, it is proper to premise some Considerations.

AND first of all, the central nitrous Spirit does every where transpire and exhale towards the Surface, to recruit the Consumptions of Nature, and for other Purposes hereafter to be mentioned. From this saline Origin straining through the Bowels of the Earth, it is by every one understood Vegetation is carried on; and that the Light and vital Warmth of the Sun is impregnated by it through the whole Region of Air; and the mutual Intercourses or Operations upon one another[38] between the Sun's Rays, and these saline Exhalations, by a Kind of Magnetism between them, is too obvious in a Multitude of Instances to want any Comment.

I know in nothing indeed where there is a greater Intercourse and Sympathy; and a considerable Illustration of which may be made by the following Experiment. If any one in the Spring-time, when the Sun is approaching nearer to us, digs up a Piece of Earth, and after Infusion and Filtration, evaporates the Liquor, he will find at the Bottom of the Vessel a Sixth Part of Salt more than at any other Time of the Year, from the same Quantity of Earth managed after the same Manner; the nitrous Salt for many Reasons not arising in so great a Quantity for the Exigencies of Nature, at any other Times; whence I conceive it manifestly to prove, that there is such an Efflux of this Salt as before suggested, and a Kind of Sublimation of it into the Air, and that this saline Spirit hath a Sort of Sympathy with the superior Heat. But that we may not use more Arguments than are necessary to prove the Energy of this Principle, every one who is doubtful herein may observe,[39] that not only Plants are produced and nourished by its subtle and luxuriant Insinuation into their Fibres, but also from the same aerial Spirit the Life of Animals, and even the humane Species is preserved. And I cannot see any Difficulty in the Opinion, that the best Temperature of the Blood and animal Juices, the Renewal of wasted Spirits, the Restauration of Strength, and the good and healthful Constitution of the Viscera, Members, and whole Body, is maintained by the Assistance of this nitro-aerial Spirit. Nor does any Thing appear more congruous to Reason, than that from the same Cause does the Racy Spirit of the Blood arise, as it is not derivable from any other; nor is it my single Opinion, that from the same Principle it derives its Colour; but as there are no Arguments even objected to this Doctrine, it is needless to imploy more Time in its Vindication.

BUT further, it may happen that this nitro-aerial Spirit may various Ways be changed in its Properties; that is, either with Regard to its prolifick Influences, (if it may be so expressed) or, which much[40] oftner happens, in its accidental and adventitious Impurities.

SOMETIMES this universal Principle languishes and degenerates, and in its own productive Womb is tainted with somewhat pernicious to Vitality, and that natural balsamick Constitution of Blood that supports it; and as often as this is the Case, the whole

Orders of living Beings may look upon it as War declared against them: But where any Alteration is made upon it by particular and fortuitous Causes, it is generally from too much Humidity diluting it, as in immoderate and unseasonable Rains, whence moist, crude, and unwholsome Vapours exhale; for every one knows how much Humidity is a Promoter of Putrefaction; whence Swarms of Insects, which is a certain Forerunner of a Pestilence: It also sometimes happens, that this vital Spirit, which so much delights in Dryness, is almost quite extinguished by a rainy Season; in which Exigency, what Miseries may not Mankind expect, when a small Change is of so fatal Consequence? This is abundantly confirmed by the Experience of Marshy Countries, where the Diseases recurring every Year are very41 fatal, by means of the putrid and damp Exhalations.

FURTHERMORE, this nitrous Principle may be sometimes changed in its own Repository by too intense a Heat from within, as well as without; for by so precipitate a Sublimation its Spirit may be deadned; that is, being robbed of its balsamick Quality, (which is no Absurdity to suppose) and kindled into too rapid a Motion, it may receive a kind of *Empyreuma*; and from which Adustion there may arise several Sorts of Distemperature; as Blasts upon Trees, and Diseases amongst Cattle; and at last end in a Pestilence amongst Mankind.

FOR further Illustration hereof it may be observed, that the nitrous Spirit which circulates through the subterraneous Caverns may, instead of Obtaining a further Purification, take along with it corrupt and poysonous Vapours from arsenical or other Minerals; and loaded therewith, break out into the open Air: And this we have confirmed from common Observation in the Western Climes of *Africa*, that lye under the *Equator*, wherein the very42 Showers seem to be endued with a Stiptick or Caustick Power, so as to taint the Cloaths and Skin of the Travellers, and burn, as it were, upon them pestilential Characters. From which Disposition it cannot be a Wonder to any, that the Plague should reign after Earthquakes; because a poysonous Spirit at such Times break out into the Air; as also that Nitre thus loaded with an impure Mixture, and sometimes too that which is deadly, should of it self, like the Occursion of an Acid, force out its Way wherever there is Room, and leave behind in its Passage many Marks of Malignity; so that subterraneous Animals, such as Moles, Mice, Serpents, Conies, Foxes,&c. as conscious of approaching Mischief, leave their Burrows, and lie open in the Air; which is also a certain Sign of a Pestilence at Hand: Hence also a sudden Death of Fish; and a Departure of the Birds of the Air, to secure their Safety in that which is more wholesome.

AFTER these Observations, it remains to shew how the nitrous Spirit frequently receives a Change like to that which may be termed Corruption, although it is vulgarly accounted incorruptible in it self,43 and is serviceable in Preserving other Things from Putrefaction.

TO the Solution of this uncommon Difficulty, it is to be taken Notice that Corruption here is not in that Sense strictly as when it is the Produce of Humidity, but somewhat more congruous to the peculiar Nature of a nitrous Spirit; which although it cannot, like some other Bodies, putrifie, yet if it can be changed from its Nature and Figure, so as not to be reducible into them again, it does not seem improperly said that such a Change is equivalent to Corruption, its Vitality or Essence being destroyed, and a new Texture being obtained. And this I shall further endeavour to illustrate by a double Argument.

FIRST, It is not at all to be doubted, but that what Art, which is the Imatator of Nature, can do, may be done by the Efficiency of a more powerful Agent; and the most expert Chymists do shew a certain Corruption of Salt; nor would it be any great Labour to discover here the Method how it is done, were it not a Crime to expose the Secrets of Nature on44 trifling Occasions. But if my Authority is not sufficient to support an Assertion of this Weight, I trust no one will reject the Conviction that arises from Effects, and therefore I shall restrain the Proof hereof to as short a Compass as possible. As then it is established by the concurrent Authority of Antiquity, that as Fire, as it is an Element capable of Degeneration, and seemingly of Corruption, may increase a pestilential Malignity by Means of its great Subtilty, its prodigious Increase, and swift Propagation; Qualities too which a Pestilence very much partakes of. That which they conceited of Fire, seems to me to be applicable in a much more philosophical Sense to that Spirit we are speaking of, and which so nearly resembles it. I am indeed a Stranger to any Thing in the Universe that makes so swift a Progress as a Pestilence, and therefore the infectious *Miasmata* are in the sacred Scriptures styled *Arrows that fly in the Dark*; and howsoever certain are their Strokes, and tho' by Means of their Fineness they penetrate into the very Marrow, they yet shun by their Subtilty our Conceptions.

A S to the spreading of a Contagion from one to another, and so on to Thousands, there is nothing can be possibly more swift in the Progress of Fire; and it exceeds even *Antimony* in the Retention of its Properties, though that loses them not in a thousand Infusions: But the instantaneous Progress of this Enemy to Mankind is best illustrated by the Rapidity of Light, which is not greater. But more of this we pass by till we come professedly to speak of a Contagion.

S E C O N D L Y, the particular Nature of the pestilential *Miasmata*, may be known from their peculiar Influence upon the saline Particles in a humane Body; for nothing acts with more Efficacy and Energy upon a saline Body, than another partaking of the same Quality; and nothing is more plain than that this nitrous Spirit is of more Efficacy than the *Alkahest* it self, as by it the fibrous Parts of the Blood are immediately corroded and dissolved; and therefore after dangerous Hemorrhages, very little Coagulation can be obtained in the extravasated Blood, unless by its being exposed to the Cold: but as often as that does happen, do not we immediately find a Fixation of the Fluids, and a certain Congelation of the Juices, which greatly retards their rapid Motions, and sometimes brings even a total Stagnation: It's furthermore of considerable Importance to our present Argument, that Spasms, the constant Attendants of a Plague, have their Origin from an acrid vellicating Salt in the nervous Fluid.

T O these it may likewise be added, that a Pestilence has a great Similitude to a scorbutick Habit, having its Origin from a saline Constitution of Blood; and the great Likeness there is in many Circumstances of their Generation and Propagation, insomuch that after a Pestilence is with others ceased, it will yet continue to infect scorbutick Constitutions; as hereafter will further appear: From the same Cause likewise does a pestilential Contagion reign most in Maritime Countries, and near the Sea-Coasts; because such a saline Disposition does there most abound; and the Truth of this, the Maritime Parts of our own Country do by sad Experience too much testifie.

L A S T L Y, If Arguments taken to this Purpose from the Method of Cure were valid, from thence it may be gathered, that a saline Spirit hath a great share in giving Rise to a Pestilence; for in our curative Regards for this Distemper, a skilful and upright Physician bends his whole Care at first to prevent its Attack, which he does by the Use of oleaginous Substances, by that Means expecting to cover over the Stomach as it were with a Plaster, to guard it against sharp and corrosive *Effluvia*; the same Intention is also pursued by Medicines, in endeavouring to defend against the poysonous Taint, or throw it out when received by Alexipharmicks and Diaphoreticks: For every one who is but tolerably conversant in such Practice, very well knows that the saline Particles are thrown off this Way much more effectually than by any other; and a further Demonstration of this Matter is also, that the Sweat of infected Persons, as in the late Sickness, gives extream pungent Pains by its Acrimony in its Exit; and that the more brackish such Sweat comes out, the more serviceable it proves; whereas when it happened to be soft and insipid, it was a sure Forerunner of worse Symptoms, and even of Death.

F U R T H E R M O R E, as to curative Intentions, all Diligence was used to preserve and restore the internal Ferments from a Contagion; and this was chiefly done by saline Preparations of various Kinds, which gave greater Energy to the natural Spirits, so as to alter and renew them by Means of that Similitude of Texture and Constitution naturally between them.

A G A I N, what was excreted did greatly establish this our Hypothesis; what was thrown up by hard Vomiting discovered nothing more than a rancid Brackishness, that vellicated the Stomach into Convulsions by its acrimonious and corrosive Qualities; and the frothy and fermentative Nature of what was ejected by Stool, fully showed its saline Mixture: But we shall come more fully to talk of this hereafter: To conclude therefore this Controversie; although the Hypothesis here laid down may at first Appearance seem new, yet it does not so far differ from the Sentiments of the Ancients upon the same Subject, as confirm49 and explain what they have said: It comes down to us for the Opinion of some of them, that a Putrefaction of Choler in an humane Body gives Rise to a Pestilence; and of others, that Fire may be so corrupted, as to occasion the same; what therefore the former conceived of Choler, and the latter of Fire, we judge more justly ascribed here to a vitiated saline Spirit. But least we should too long dwell upon this Argument, if it was needful to recite all the Causes enumerated by Authors of this Malady, it would be difficult to find any one which does not coincide with this our Hypothesis; so that whosoever pleases to be at this Pains, must either assent with us, or reject them; and he that does not like our Opinion, would do well to shew a better.

IN the above-described Pestilence, as indeed in many others, Persons frequently died, without any preceeding Symptoms of Horror, Thirst, or concomitant Fever: For the Confirmation of which, I shall give an Instance or two out of a great many; A Woman, who was the only one left alive of the Family, and yet to her Thinking perfectly well, perceived upon her Breast50 the pestilential Spots, which she looking upon to be the fatal Tokens, in a very short Space died, without feeling any other Disorder, or any other Forerunner of Death.

A Youth also of a good Constitution, after he had found himself on a sudden marked with the Tokens of the Contagion, believed at first they were not the genuine Marks, because he found himself so well, and yet he was dead in less than four Hours after, as his Physician had before prognosticated.

BUT how suddenly soever the Sickness killed some People, whether by suddenly seizing the Brain, Heart, Lungs, or any other principal Part, with a deadly Infection, or poisoning the vital Spirits at once, so that no Appearance could be discerned, even of a lurking Fever, yet for the most Part, some Fever did shew it self.

AND it cannot be thought strange, that most who took the Contagion should have a Fever, to those who consider the Nature of a nitrous Spirit, especially when degenerated, and that from the most slight51 Cause it will take Fire, and excite Heat; and the Fever accompanying this present Sickness was of the worst Kind, both on Account of its State and Periods, sometimes imitating a Quotidian, and at others a Tertian; sometimes seeming to retreat, and at others attacking again with redoubled Fury: There was never a total Cessation, but sometimes a Remission for an Hour or two, although every Exacerbation was worse than the former; but this I pass by here, having Occasion hereafter to enlarge further thereupon.

AT length therefore, to discharge my Promise in giving a short Account of a Contagion, as of a Disease that is communicable that Way only, and killing most it seizes, it is to be taken Notice, that the Infection of the pestilential Poison is not only transferrable from one Subject to another, either by mediate or immediate Contact, and exciting the same Symptoms; but all the Conditions likewise of its Exertion, are as conspicuous as the Noon-day Sun; wherefore those Arguments to prove the pestilential Corruption not to arise from Contagion, are trifling and not worth Notice, as altogether disconsonant to Reason52 and Experience; as after I have enumerated the Conditions of a contagious Exertion, I doubt not but to make this Matter clear to every one.

FOUR Things chiefly are necessary to a Contagion:

FIRST, That there is an Efflux of the contagious *Seminium*.

SECONDLY, That there is a convenient *Medium* for the contagious Particles to move through, and be conveyed by.

THIRDLY, A Fitness in the Subject to receive and cherish the contagious *Effluvia*. And,

FOURTHLY, A due Stay of this *Seminium*; of all which distinctly.

THE Quantity of Necessaries daily taken in for Refreshment does evidently demonstrate, that insensible Perspiration is much larger than all other Evacuations together: But where a Pestilence invades, a yet much greater Wast is made that Way than in a Time of Health, by the53intestine Colluctation and Struggle of opposite Principles in the animal

Fluids; this is confirmed by the Observation of *Sanctorius*, who tells us, that Persons taken with a pestilential Contagion, immediately become much lighter, the *Effluvia* of their Bodies breaking through on all Sides with Rapidity; for such is the Energy of the pestilential Taint, that it immediately subtilizes more thick Substances, and gives them such a Sharpness, as to cut their Way like so many Needles, or Wedges, and very often carry along with them those natural Spirits which should be a Preservative to the whole Frame: Hence sometimes follow Swoonings and Faintings that are fatal, and Indications of that Wast of Spirits that hath been made by the pestilential Poison.

H E N C E moreover it appears, of what a diffused Nature this Contagion may be of, by the great Plenty that transpires from an infected Person; and which Steam alone, as it is sufficient to communicate the Infection, so it is also capable of vast Dilatation and Diffusion; not much unlike the Snuff of a Candle, which not only emits a great deal of Smoak, but carries54 a considerable Stench along with it into very distant Parts.

S E C O N D L Y , A fit *Medium* is very conducive to the Propagation of the Plague; for according to the Disposition of that, in being more or less open or confined, is the Infection sooner or slower communicated: Nor is there any Doubt, but that the Air is this fit*Medium*, and whose Pores, altho' very minute, are readily filled with it; and therein the noxious *Effluria* lodge securely, unless expelled by any external Force.

T H E Air is moreover the more convenient Recepticle and Conveyance of this pestilential Poyson, on account of that nitrous Spirit with which it abounds; hence it more easily receives the poisonous*Aura*, and faithfully preserves it as in a proper Conservatory, and on this Account the pernicious Qualities, (unless first destroyed by some uncommon Power) sooner reach any Subject to act upon, and float about in Readiness for Destruction: Sometimes also the pestilential*Miasmata* may be broke and destroyed by the Occursion of others,55without any Perception of either having been in this *Medium*.

H E N C E it comes strongly to be conjectured, how the pestilential*Seminium* comes to be hid so secretly in the Porosities of the Air, so as to be conveyed from one Country to another, and to travel unperceived into very distant Regions. Further, as this *Medium* is more still, it is so much the more capable to receive the pestilential Infection; whereupon Places that are close, confined, and dark, as Prisons, and Houses in Vallies, are much more liable to Contagion, than Situations upon Eminencies, where the Air is frequently agitated by Winds; for the malignant *Effluria* cannot so well fix in an Air so tumultuously hurried about; and they are likewise rendred less hurtful by a continual Mixture of fresh Air with them.

T H I R D L Y , A suitable Disposition of the Subject is very necessary for the Reception of the pestilential Taint; and this Disposition respects either some Fitness in the Pores of the Body, or a long Accumulation of distempered Humours. The more open the Pores are, and the wider,56 by so much the more easily will the Infection penetrate into the Body; and the more constringed they are, the better Security is there against it, insomuch that hardly by any other Means can it enter.

A Turgescency of bad Humours greatly facilitates the Plague's Admission into any Person, whether such a morbid Constitution arises from the Suppression of usual Evacuations, or from an erroneous Use of the Non-naturals; and most of all, a Load of bad Humours from an Excess or a Surfeit, leaves so great a Similitude to the pestilential Poison, as greatly to encourage its Admission. But besides these Dispositions of the Subject, it is much to the Purpose to suggest this following Observation, that the Plague is sometimes so much hereditary, and influenced by a seminal Taint, that in a common Contagion it shall much exert it self in some in the same Manner upon Children, as their Parents, as in the *Small-Pox*, and other Affections of like Nature.

F O U R T H L Y , It is necessary that there should be a continual Lodgment of the pestilential Poison; for if the noxious Steams57 were blown away as soon as received, there would be but little Mischief done; but those which meet with any glutinous Matter, and a certain*Lentor* from the Viscidity of the Humours, with which they lie entangled, until they are carried through the larger Vessels with the Blood, begin to fuse and taint all the animal Juices; and thus the pestiferous *Miasmata* having got Possession, are able to subvert the whole Machine, and bring all into Confusion, without requiring any long Stay to execute their pernicious Effects; for as soon as they once find a viscid and tenacious Substance, they eagerly join with it, and are but with great Difficulty to be extricated. Yet notwithstanding it is generally thus, I have sometimes found Instances of a longer Stay of the pestilential Poison before its Exertion, where the Symptoms of Infection have not appeared until a fit Time of Maturity for Eruption into Action, and for the Confirmation of which several Instances might be produced were it controverted; I have known many go into the Country after Intercourses with the infected, and keep well for a Month or two, when the Enemy that has lay hid so long, rushed out[58] of its Fastnesses, and by its Fury sufficiently compensated its foregoing Delays; and this Eruption sooner might very probably have been hindred, partly by the Viscosity of the Humours entangling the pestilential *Miasmata*, and partly from an over-powerful balsamick Quality, natural to a good Blood, and to a Plenty and Vigour of animal Spirit; but as I would not be tedious upon Things so very obvious, this shall suffice concerning a Contagion.

BESIDES the Causes already recited, there may be others also worth Consideration, *viz*. the eating corrupted, or rotten Flesh; and it is not at all foreign to our Purpose here to take Notice, that on the Year before the late pestilential Sickness, there was a great Mortality amongst the Cattel, from a very wet Autumn, whereby their Carcases were sold amongst the ordinary People at a very mean Price; and a great deal of putrid Humours in all likelihood produced from thence: And this, in the Opinion of many, was the Source of our last Calamities; and many knowing Persons ascribe the Pestilence to this Origin, as the morbid Disposition which such a Feeding must needs subject the People,[59] could not but facilitate both the Infection and Progress of that fatal Destroyer.

TO this I do not deny, but that the common People, who fed upon such a Diet even to Gluttony, might treasure up Matter enough for so deadly an Impression, and with which the Plague might naturally enough go into a Co-operation; but such Provision, although very much corrupt, and liable thereby to excite Symptoms like to those in a Pestilence; yet they were not in Plenty enough to supply the whole Market, and therefore a Cause so private and particular, could not be supposed to extend to so universal an Effect.

HENCE it is further manifest, that a corrupt Diet can do no more in giving a pestilential Impression, than a good one can in removing it; and therefore, not to dwell too long upon this Matter, it is my Opinion that such a Way of Living may raise the Humours to a Degree of Putrefaction, as brings Fevers very malignant, and causes epidemical Diseases, but not a true Pestilence.

[60]

AND the Conjecture that a Sickness amongst Cattle is transferable to the humane Species, hath not yet appeared on any good Foundation; but to remove this Difficulty, no one doubts but that a Plague amongst Cattle, from some common Cause, as a Corruption of the aerial Nitre, and which differs from a Plague amongst Men but in Degree, may also be transmitted to the humane Species; that is, a feebler Degree of Poison, and a milder *Aura*, may taint the Herbage, than that which is sufficient to destroy the firmer Constitution of Animals; besides which, from the Diversity in the Pores of Brutes, and their different Constitutions, and the Fortitude in the Spirit of a Man, I cannot be induced to believe that the Pestilence amongst Cattle from a private Cause, can ever obtain any Dominion over Mankind. These Stories therefore have no Weight with me, that a certain Leech, upon opening an Horse, that with a great many others had died of some common Distemper, in Order to know what it was, and finding certain pestilential Tokens upon his Inwards, both the Master and the Family soon died of the Infection; which[61] yet went no further than that Family, but expired with them.

DURING the late Plague likewise at *London*, a Citizen travelling into the Country, found his Horse of a sudden to tire and fall down, whereupon he opened his Mouth to find out if possible the Cause of so sudden a Change; when the good Man, upon Receipt of the Horse's Breath upon him, immediately grew sick, and died in two Days Time.

BUT these and the like Instances certainly tend to prove no more than that there may be Constitutions and malignant Steams, which, by agitating the Mass of Humours, may excite putrid and irregular Orgasms, wherein the Juices and Animal Fluids, according to the Quantity and Prevalency of the Distemperature, and the Variety of the infused Taint, with the Diversity of Putrefaction, goes into Corruption; but the forementioned Transplantation of the Plague does not happen but where there is a suitable Predisposition of Humours to admit it, as its Cause is not general.

62

MOREOVER, although the Intemperance of the Year, sudden Change of Air, Suppression of usual Evacuation, Diminution of Perspiration, Drunkenness, Venery, and Passions of the Mind, especially Anger and Fear, are justly reckoned amongst the remote Causes of a Pestilence; yet they regard rather the Invasion of it, than its Origin; but of this we shall say more hereafter. As to the above-mentioned Passions, it is almost incredible how some, at the Height of the Infection, would from a very slight Cause kindle into the utmost Rage, and rave at one another like meer Scolds, until Death parted their Contentions.

NOR does Fear or Sorrow less prepare the Way for the Infection, by deadning the Fancy and Memory, by Suffocating the Spirits, Suppressing the natural Heat, breaking the Constitution, and Promoting Malignity: We have manifold Instances of this kind in Readiness; but if, as some do, we should be prolix in the Enumeration of Things that want not Proof, the Reader would be quite tired with needless Stories.

63

BUT now it may be convenient to add a few Remarks concerning the Translation of a Pestilence from an hot Country to a cold one; for according to the different Effects of Heat and Cold, the one attenuating and rarefying, the other condensing and constipating, the pestilential Venom is strangely altered, insomuch that in a Thing so obvious, there does not require much to be said: Every Thing of this kind prodigiously spreads in hot Climates, as being more subtile than even the Air it self; tho' the same in the Northern Countries is more restrained, and confined in Fastnesses it cannot escape from; and from hence the Reason is very obvious why there is so much Difference between the Diseases of different Climates, which would be too tedious for us here to go into.

TO come nearer therefore to our Business; the same Affections that in an hot Country heat the Blood and other Juices, so as in a great Measure to put them into Fusion, when translated into the contrary Extream may give contrary Properties to the same Fluids, and è contra; and this might be demonstrated by innumerable 64 Experiments, were there any Doubt about it.

IT being then granted, that this Plague first was brought from *Africa*, or *Asia*, to *Holland*, and from thence into *Britain*, every one may easily conjecture, how much Alteration it must undergo in such a Travel, from a hot and dry Climate into a moist and cold one, not so much in its own Nature, as from the Vehicle of Air which conveyed it, and thereby producing different Degrees of Infection, and Series of Symptoms: But this Variation would be most discernable in the Complication of the pestilential *Seminium*, with the particular Diseases of each Country, and those which are as it were peculiar to them: This in our Case is very well worth Notice, for in *Holland*, where the Scurvy extreamly reigns, and therefore, for Reasons before given, most liable to a pestilential Infection, it obtained only as a more aggravated Scurvy, as shall hereafter be further remarked.

AS for that Opinion of the famous *Kircher*, about animated Worms, I must confess I never could come at any such 65 Discovery with the Help of the best Glasses, nor ever found the same discovered by any other; but perhaps in our cloudy Island we are not so sharp-sighted as in the serene Air of *Italy*; and with Submission to so great a Name, it seems to me very disconsonant to Reason, that such a pestilential *Seminium*, which is both of a nitrous and poisonous Nature, should produce a living Creature.

AS in putrid Fevers, so in a Pestilence, Malignity is a Destroyer of Insects, and frightens them away as it were alive, so far is it from giving Birth to them; indeed in some malignant Ulcers and Cancers, and in the Blood of some People, sometimes *animalcula* are found; which is rather to be looked upon as the Effect of some Fault in the nutritious Juice, than the Produce of any Poison; and therefore they are not to be accounted amongst the Causes of a Pestilence.

66

SECTION III.

Of the primary Seat of a Pestilence; where, by the Way, is considered the Nature of the Spirits, and their Infection in an humane Body from Poison.

IN Order to put an End to the Controversies about the Seat of a Pestilence, which have from Antiquity even to this Day been warmly maintained, many Authors putting the Heart for the Principle of Life and Death, some the Brain, and others the Stomach, Lungs, or Liver: It will be necessary here to discover the immediate Residence of the pestilential *Seminium*. Since therefore the above-mentioned *Aura*, according to Hypothesis, is very subtile and spirituous, for that Reason there must necessarily be some conformable Property in the Matter which is fit to receive it; as therefore there is not in the whole humane Machine any Subject more apposite, and capable of its Union, than the animal Spirits, we must fix its Residence there. But because I am sensible what Objections this Opinion lies open to, with some Persons, who may not conceive how an immediate[67] Infection of the Spirits is communicable to the Viscera, and all Parts of the Body, it will be necessary to go thro' this Matter in a very particular Manner, by enquiring;

FIRST, What are the Spirits concerning which we are here speaking?

SECONDLY, What is that Disposition of Spirits which makes them fit to receive the pestilential Impression? And,

THIRDLY, After what Manner the vitiated Spirits can affect the whole Body with Disorders?

TO this Purpose we must know, that the Spirits are the most thin and subtile Particles of the Aliment and other Juices, raised to the utmost Perfection and Volatility by the innate Heat, and the nitro-aerial Spirit, to serve in the Operations of the Mind, and all the Purposes of the animal OEconomy.

THE Matter whence the Spirits are generated is the Chyle, and their Restauration, Confirmation, and Vigour, from the[68] Recruits of Food, as is their Languor, Prostration, and utter Extinction from the Want of it; so that howsoever they were first generated in the original, they owe their Conservation and Vitality to the Nourishment continually brought in; and although in a State of perfect Health *they* are never changed by *that*, yet they continually act upon that after various Ways, bringing it from a crude, recrementicious State, into a noble Juice, or rich spiritual Balsam, retaining its ideal Character: And hence it comes about, that although there is a daily Waste of Spirits, there is no Want, because Nature is continually, while Things are in Health, making more; insomuch that after a due Constitution of Spirits is obtained, they of themselves are the main Efficients in making more, as one Light is kindled by another, and as the Blood it self is the chief Instrument in Sanguification, or making more Blood.

IT is a Matter indeed of much more Difficulty to determine, how Particles from a gross Origin, should be raised to so great Volatility and Fineness; but this is very certain, that when they are elaborated in the most perfect Manner, they exceed even[69] the Light and Activity of the Sun-Beams; and the brighter and more active they are, the better do they perform their Offices in the OEconomy, as from their Efficiency is procured a State of Health and Vigour both in Body and Mind.

IT is of no great Moment to enquire, what Quantity of Spirit is necessary for the Conservation and Support of an humane Body, so that we do but know they partake of the Source from whence they are generated, insomuch that they are more or less perfect, according to the greater or lesser Degree of Purity in their productive Juices.

BUT I must here acknowledge my self diffident in that Opinion of the Spirits being prepared of a different Nature for particular Parts, for according to the Influences of the Mind, and the Contiguity, Rectitude, or Consent of the Vessels, they are by a voluntary Act determined the same into this or that Limb or Part: Which is manifest enough in the Prick of a Needle, or a venomous Bite, from the great Affluence of Spirits to that Part; I have therefore no Notion of a continued Emanation[70] of Spirits, but that on such Occasions they are called, by the Sensation upon the affected Part, from the nervous Origin where they are elaborated.

SECONDLY, It sometimes happens that the Spirits degenerate from their native Purity, as also at others that they prove abortive, in not arriving to their utmost Maturity, whereby they lie more open to foreign Impressions of Distemperature.

BUT when the juices, or common Promptuary from whence the Spirits are generated, is not uniform, genuine, and perfect in kind, it is impossible that Spirits should be made from it in any tolerable Perfection; for one may as well pretend to wash a Brick, or draw clear Water from a foul Spring, as expect pure and natural Spirits from a corrupt and vitiated Chyle; although even when the Chyle is in right Order, there may various Errors happen in the Generation of Spirits, as from too great an Heat agitating the Blood in a preternatural Manner, or from an imperfect or unequal Separation of Particles, or from too much Cold causing an Intermixture of Crudities; and again, although the Spirits[71] are duly elaborated, yet they may run into irregular Motions, and be the Occasion of many Disorders: But what is most to the Purpose, they may sometimes also receive a Taint from external Impressions.

AND this Aptitude, or Propensity of the Spirits to receive a pestilential Taint, is manifest from their fiery, or rather saline Nature, for on Account of that Subtilty which they acquire thereby, do they more naturally attract the contagious *Aura*, than Bodies more gross and heavy: For as these Spirits, as before observed, are nitrous, and inflammable, by their Similitude to a pestilential *Aura*, they not only are fitted to receive, but even attract it, and provoke it into Union; as the Snuff of a Candle just blown out, if it is not too far off, will by an Affinity of Qualities be soon rekindled by another lighted one at some Distance; and how much soever the poisonous Qualities of the pestilential *Effluvia* may be destructive of the animal Spirits, yet there is nothing more certain, than that their Taint is very easily impressed upon them.

[72]

AFTER the pestilential Poison is thus received by the Spirits, it is impossible to express the fatal Consequences, and the cruel Havock that is made in the whole OEconomy; for the same Instruments which before were aery, lucid, and like the Rays of the Sun, immediately become vapid, dark, and useless, neither able to invigorate the Constitution, nor defend it against the Contagion.

THIRDLY, Having briefly passed over these Matters, it remains that we shew by what Steps the humane Frame comes to be disordered by this pestilential Invasion; and in Order to this, I know not a more fatal Circumstance in Nature than to have the very Guards and tutelary Preservers of Life, turn, as it were, Deserters and Betrayers. For there is nothing more manifest, than that the whole Compage, and its several Parts, run into Decay as soon as the pestilential Taint takes Place; for immediately upon the first Seizure, the whole Effort of Nature, as at *Rome* when *Hannibal* was at their Gates, is recollected against the Enemy, as sensible that all is at Stake, but being unequal to the Conflict,[73] they retreat, and are taken Prisoners, leaving the whole Body defenceless. Hence the Infection runs through all the Blood, whereby the Heart and Lungs are principal Sufferers. Hence such a Corruption of the nutritive Fluids, that the whole nervous System is disturbed, the burning Heat of the *Pancreas* produces the most extream Sickness, and hence follows such a Depravation of the whole Machine, that all the vital Faculties cease to act, and Death closes the fatal Scene.

BUT I do not at all see how such a noble Part as the Heart, should be first affected by any particular specifick Quality in the Poison of a Plague, to affect that more than any other; as if it was so frightful, as some would have it, to attack the Principles of Life at once; for the Heart seems at first to be affected chiefly from the Multiplicity of Vessels, and the great Crowd of Circulation that Way, giving Opportunity for the Venom sooner to arrive thither; concerning which we shall have Occasion to say more under that Head of Symptoms.

[74]

UPON the strong, presumptive Proofs therefore that the pestilential Poison chiefly resides in the Spirits, we cannot but much admire at the Weakness of those, who expect to detect its Nature and Cause from what they can find on the Dissection of morbid

Bodies, and such like Circumstances: For a very noted Person, and one of exquisite Skill in Anatomy, although he himself at last fell in the general Calamity, affirmed, that the Seat of the last Pestilence was in the extream Angles of the *Plexus Choroides*, towards the *Cerebellum*, because he had found a small Vesicle there; others have observed the Lungs to have been marked with the Tokens of Infection; others report the Heart to have been tumefied, and burnt as it were, to a Coal; whereas it is plain, that these Parts are only so many Fields of Battle, where the Spirits and the Infection contend it with each other; Nor will any one, who rightly considers these Things, wonder, that such Marks of Devastation should every where be left by so cruel an Enemy.

THEREFORE, although it should be granted that the most obvious and open Tokens of a Pestilence are from a spiritual and an invisible Cause, and whose Effects may perhaps sometimes be laid open to Sight, yet I have no Intention to discourage anatomical Dissections as a needless Trouble, for by such Light, Medicine is recovered from the Reproach of Conjecture; but when Bodies are opened which have been destroyed by such subtile Agents as here spoke of, there is no Confidence to be given from thence to the Nature of the Disease; and those who have been most knowing in the Nature, Use, and Disorders of the Spirits, very well can direct how to recover those Disorders, and avoid future Inconveniencies by immediate Application thereunto.

AND Lastly, to conclude this Doctrine concerning the Spirits Infection, this irrefragable Argument may be produced from the Intention of Cure; for I have experienced by more than a thousand Instances, that the more cardiack and alexipharmick Medicines are subtile and spirituous, the more certainly do they encounter the pestilential Poison with Success; whereas, on the contrary, those Medicines which are coarser and slower of Exertion, do little or no Good. But this we refer to the curative Part hereafter in another Section.

SECTION IV.

Of the Complication of a Pestilence with other Distempers, and particularly with the Scurvy.

AS the Pestilence is the most powerful of all other Distempers, so it also claims a particular Privilege of joining with all others; so that it does not more excel in its own Contrariety and Antipathy to Nature, than it asserts a Prerogative over all those various Evils which the humane Frame is subjected to, and draws them into its Assistance in exercising its cruel Power over Mankind.

THIS Assertion might be supported by a Multitude of Instances, if it were not for taking up too much of the Reader's Time; for which Reason we shall only take Notice, that amongst all those Distempers which are thus inclined to join their Forces with this most powerful Enemy, some seem to have a more particular Fitness for such a Union, from a common Affinity in the Nature of their Infection, and the Energy of their Poison.

ONE of the First of this Class is the venereal Disease, with which the pestilential Venom does in a very familiar Manner unite it self. At the first breaking out indeed of the last Sickness it was given out by common Fame, that those who were previously infected with any foul Distemper, as the Pox in particular, would be secured thereby against the pestilential Taint; but wicked and impious was the Consequence of such a Suggestion; for many were hereby encouraged to seek the most lascivious and filthy Prostitutions, on purpose to be secur'd by one previous Infection against another: But besides the poisonous Quality peculiar to this nasty Disease, besides that Expence of Spirit in the procuring it, and besides a lost Force of the Constitution thereby, the greatest Aggravation to this Misfortune was, that the very Taint which was to defend against another, had it in its Nature to be more forcibly attracted by it; so that the rash Adventurer was soon brought to a bitter Repentance for his Experiment, by sinking immediately under the pestilential Contagion at its first Stroke; and it was common to find, by a very easy Transition, the venereal Buboes changed into pestilential Carbuncles, except in a few Instances where Nature found out an uncommon Artifice against these united Powers, by endeavouring an Ejectment of their joint Malignities by Salivation, whereby sometimes the Patient was brought into some Chance for his Life, both the Poisons being in a great Measure cast off together that way.

B U T here it may not be improper to admonish the young Physicians not to be too forward Imitators of Nature in such a Circumstance; unless they will run the same Hazard with a certain Empirick, who crouded his Powders upon the Sick that raised an untimely spitting, and brought a great many into a dangerous Condition, which by a regular Practice might have been, tho' with Difficulty, saved.

Yet to set this whole Affair in a clear Light, there is great Reason to suspect that in many Cases Mercury had for some time remained in the Body, which,79 like a Snake in the Grass, being raised by the Pestilential Infection, flew up into a Salivation; for the febrile Heat, assisted with Medicines also of an hot Nature, throw up the Mercury, which had long lain quiet, like a Sublimation; which should be a Caution, not only to young Physicians, but those of more standing in Practice, not to be so buisy with mercurial Medicines, to Children as well as grown Persons, as they are too much apt to be; least besides the Inconveniencies already mentioned they cause malignant Ulcers, and Rotenness upon the Bones, as it is too commonly observed to be done in irregular Practice, to the irreparable Detriment of the Patients.

I am not however ignorant that sometimes the Pestilential Venom may tumifie the salival Glands without any other Assistance, and occasion Ulcers in the Mouth as with Mercury; for it is a common Case in many malignant Fevers.

B U T it is so clear a Matter that the Pestilential and venereal Poysons may intimately join together by their Affinity with one another, to the great Detriment80 of Mankind, as to want no further Proofs to confirm it; nor does their Opinion at all obviate ours, who place the venereal Poyson in Humidity, and that of a Pestilence in Dryness, as long as the Symptoms and Affections of both discover one common Principle, that is, somewhat saline; but yet if this should not be granted, they are naturally enough joined together by their known Malignity and Destruction to human Nature.

B U T the Affinity between a Pestilence and a Scurvy is not a slight, and a supposititious Conjecture, but strengthened and confirmed by a plain Union between them, whereby they attack like confederate Troops; and both confess the same Origin, *viz*. a saline Principle; as is most remarkably obvious in their eager Coalition, whether we consider the forementioned Transplantation of the like Plague from *Turky* to *Holland*, where their Alliance was first formed; Or whether we reflect upon them both as Distempers equally epidemical, which when joined make such cruel Havock among the human Species; as neighbouring Flames catch together from a like Affinity of Parts, and burn with united Fury.

81

F O R although there is a great Difference in Salts of different Kinds, yet there is a common Property amongst them all, that when joined together they cannot hardly by any Means possibly be afterwards separated, for which Reason when these two Enemies of Mankind were joined, the complicated Evil was at first customarily distinguished by the *outlandish Scurvy*, which by a confederate Power had increased its Malignity to so great a Degree. But to give some apparent Facts, which irrefragably prove the natural Union between these two Origins of Mischief, it may be proper to recite some Symptoms common to them both, and first of all those Spots which were their certain Characteristicks.

T H E Spots of those in the Plague were sometimes so numerous, as to cover all the Body, of which we shall say more hereafter; and if we consider the Appearances and Conditions of the Spots in both, we shall find a very great Agreement; the pestilential Spots sometimes break out broad, at other Times more contracted, just in the same Manner as it happens in a Scurvy; and as to their Duration, sometimes they82 are longer out than at others in both; now also suddenly appear, and then again as suddenly turn in, and sometimes remain out for two or three Days together; and their Likeness in all Respects is frequently so great, that amongst the ignorant Nurses and Empiricks, sometimes the fatal Tokens of a Pestilence have been mistaken only for Scurvy Spots: As to their Colour in a Plague, as well as in a Scurvy, they are sometimes florid, resembling fresh Flea-Bites, and at others dusky and livid; and I met with them in a certain Youth resembling Violet Flowers painted all over the Body; and in some I have seen them almost quite black, which are with great Difficulty to be distinguished from the true pestilential Tokens.

THERE are other Symptoms also that denote the Agreement herein, such as large Stools, of a saline and fetid Nature, and which are with great Difficulty restrained by the most powerful Medicines; but if such a Flux continues, it threatens irretrievable Injuries, as Corrosion, Inflammation, and sometimes even Sphacelation of the Bowels, with intolerable Gripings, and sometimes Loss of Blood: Furthermore,[83] the Agreement that there is between the Ulcers and Tumours of both evidently demonstrate the Affinity of both their Origins, as will hereafter more fully appear in that Part about the Cure.

THE Pestilence likewise shews its Affinity with the Scurvy, by leaving behind it a scorbutick Habit, even where a Person was not given to it in the least before; and it is not indeed at all strange, that after such Disorders, and Corruption of the animal Juices, and such an Exhalation or Suffocation of subtile and spirituous Particles, an Habit should be confirmed, that can be removed but by the most generous Remedies, and the most powerful Antiscorbuticks.

IT remains now briefly to enquire, whether a Pestilence coming upon another Disease, in any Instances proves of Service; and this I shall dispatch in two Histories of Cases, one in a Consumption, and the other in the *King's-Evil*.

A Girl of fifteen Years of Age was so emaciated, that she had left little besides Skin and Bones, and taking no Nourishment[84] for 14 Days together, she was given over as gone, but being called to the same House, to see her Mother, and two others who had the Infection, and recovered, the same Distemper seized that Creature almost half-dead before, whom also I then attended; but she who just before lay as expiring, seemed animated by the feverish Heat, began to move her Limbs, and with the Help of Alexipharmick Medicines, although before speechless, began to complain of painful Swellings about her; but those Buboes, which I suppose would otherwise have broke out, for Want of Matter to raise them, were dissipated by Transpiration; so that she recovered, and in about two Weeks also manifestly lost her former Distemper, and gathered Flesh and Strength.

ANOTHER Maid of about 16 Years of Age had been so scrophulous from her Childhood, as to have many indurated Glands remain after all possible Means had been used to dissipate them. She at last was seized with the Contagion, and pestilential Buboes rose upon the strumous Glands, which suppurated, and let out a great Quantity of Filth; and upon her Recovery[85] from thence, her former Distemper was quite lost.

SOME gouty Persons likewise, and others accustomed to very obstinate Complaints, were, by a lucky Conjunction with this Infection, quite restored: and indeed most who were rightly managed in the Plague, and perfectly recovered of it, were afterwards, in many Respects, better in their Health than before; so that this terrible Enemy, as it was commonly fatal, so it also sometimes proved a Remedy. And thus much for the Complication of the Pestilence with other Distempers. We shall now proceed to its Symptoms.

SECTION V.

Of the manifest Signs of the late Pestilence.

IT is altogether foreign to my Design here, to enumerate all the Appearances that belong to a pestilential Constitution, because a great deal may be ascribed to Phantasie and Conjecture, as the Influence of Comets, and the Conjunctions of Planets, with others of like Nature: For what strange Notions have been broached concerning[86] this Contagion, which was imported to us from Abroad? Are the Tails of Comets always armed with pestilential Arrows? Or is the Air the more impure and unhealthful? Had we any Famine before the last Sickness? Or had we portentous Swarms of Insects like Clouds over us? No, just the contrary, as we before observed, all Things from Nature were promising and serene, and this Destroyer invaded us on a sudden from strange Countries; it is therefore of more Advantage to our Design here, to take all its concomitant Signs from its manifest Effects.

AND indeed there are not many peculiar to a pestilential Fever, as that is chiefly a Collection, or an Epitome of all other Fevers together, which in such a Confederacy are not therefore without a tedious Work to be enumerated in all their Affections; I shall therefore satisfie my self with describing such only which are most obvious to common Observation, and are met with in most infected Persons: And these for Method Sake I shall distribute into two Classes.

FIRST, The manifest Signs of Infection.

SECONDLY, The Appearances after Infection.

BUT hereunto I think it necessary to premise, that a Pestilence puts on sometimes one, and at others another Appearance, and sometimes even contrary ones, according to the Constitution or Age of the Patient, the Season of the Year, present or preceding Distempers, a faulty Way of Living, and the different Means of Communication, both with Respect to Virulence and Degree.

THE Symptoms of the first Class are Horror, Vomiting, Delirium, Dizziness, Head-ach, and Stupefaction.

OF the second, a Fever, Watching, Palpitation of the Heart, Bleeding at Nose, and a great Heat about the *Precordia*.

THE Signs more peculiar to a Pestilence, are those Pustules which the common People call *Blains*, Buboes, Carbuncles, Spots, and those Marks called *Tokens*; of all which distinctly.

I do not know indeed throughout the whole Compass of Nature, (as before it hath been frequently hinted) any Thing so subtile as the pestilential Poison, and what will penetrate the Body with so much Swiftness and Secrecy, insomuch that it is not perceived sometimes till long after its Entrance; what therefore is commonly said of its sensible Attack, and that the infected feel its first Insult as from a sudden Blow, is more the Effect of a deluded Imagination and Conjecture, than any solid Judgment; as the Populace are apt enough to frame strange Conceits out of their own Heads, and what hath long obtained amongst them is very difficult to erace.

WHEN therefore such a kind of People hath received the Notion, as was common in the late Sickness, concerning the forementioned Manner of Infection, it is no great Wonder that others likewise in general go into the Error, and take it for granted that this unmerciful Destroyer makes its Seizure in this violent Way, and therefrom wait for it as for a hidden Stroke.

ALTHOUGH I am not insensible, that some may have thus perceived its first Impression, upon taking in ungrateful and filthy Smells; for the pestilential *Seminium*, (as before observed) when it incorporates with other Bodies that are gross, fat, and viscid, may strike the Organs of Sensation very manifestly at its first Entrance.

AFTER the pestilential *Miasmata* have thus seized a Person, and the Spirits are overcome, the whole Mass of Blood, and other animal Juices, partake of the Disorder; from whence proceed Struggles not to be born, and a Train of Symptoms, of which quaking or shuddering is the chief, all of a sudden, without any manifest Cause.

THIS Symptome owes its Origin to the Conflict of Nature with the infused Malignity, whose Efforts of Resistance excite a Sense of Cold from the pestilential *Seminium*; after the same Manner as Nitre put upon the Tongue excites the same Sensation; it is also to be suspected that this Rigor may be owing to a Quality in the poysonous *Effluvia* of extinguishing the native Heat: And the Spasmodick Affections of the Nerves proceed from salt, sharp, malignant, and heterogeneous Particles rushing into the sensible Fibres, and vellicating them into involuntary Motions and Twitchings.

THE greatest Part indeed of the Infected perceived this Horror, but some of them more vehemently than others; but of the immediate Impression upon the Spirit there is no Room to doubt, nor of a consequent Degeneration of the whole Mass of Blood; although I am sensible that the Subtilty of the pestilential Taint took Place sooner or later, according to the different Degrees of Strength and Texture in the Body to resist it.

IT is certain that the fine and exquisite Contexture of the nervous System, and the Agreement and Consent of one Part with another, as well as the extraordinary Perfection of the Animal Spirits, set as Guards over such sensible Parts, could not but be affected with the

Apprehensions of Mischief, and shake and tremble, and use their Efforts to throw off the Danger; and indeed I take it further to be probable, that the pestilential Poison might be shook by such Means out of the Nerves into the[91] Muscles, and there cause Tention, Trembling, Vellication, Yawning, Stretching, and all those other Concomitants of putrid and malignant Fevers.

T H E Duration also of this Shuddering was as uncertain as its Degree, for it went off sometimes sooner, and at others later; sometimes in half an Hour, and at others, not till four or five Hours; which Difference I conjecture owing to the Quantity and Intenseness of the Malignity, as to the greater or lesser Struggles of Nature to resist it.

A S soon as this Horror could be said to terminate, for the most commonly a Nauseousness and Reaching succeeded, from whence there was such an excessive Loathing of Food, that even the Mention of it was irksome; a certain and infallible Sign of Seizure.

B E S I D E S the Nauseousness and Loathing, some were followed by grievous Vomitings, occasioned by the poisonous Quality of the Pestilence irritating and subverting the Stomach; for that, by Means of its nervous Coats, being endowed with an exquisite Sense,[92] endeavours to throw off any Thing offensive and corrosive with the utmost Efforts, and prevent the saline, pestilential Venom, if possible, from taking Place; insomuch that nothing is more certain, than that the Stomach, by this fine Contrivance of Nature, is ready also to throw off any other Thing disagreeable to it, as well as the Poison we are here speaking of.

S O M E endure hereby such a vehement and continued Irritation, that cannot be asswaged by any Remedies, how often soever repeated, and sometimes the Reaching continues after the Strength of the Patient is too far spent to throw any Thing up, whereby the Symptoms aggravate, and the pestilential Venom takes deeper Root in the Constitution.

A F T E R the principal Load of Humours at the Stomach are thrown up, a very frothy Bile, fermenting like Yest, follows, that in its Colour is greenish, and sometimes so fetid, that a Person cannot endure the Room without holding his Nose, such is the prodigious Putrefaction and Malignity in some of these Cases.

[93]

B U T where the Use of Medicines, otherwise effectual to stop the most obstinate Vomiting, proves ineffectual, and there follows a great Thirst and Heat, it gives strong Suspicion of Carbuncles in the Stomach, and immediate Death, so that the infected as it were vomit up their Souls, which (if we believe *Helmont*) have their Residence there; but this will be further spoke of in the Prognosticks.

B U T before I proceed any further, the Health of my Country, and the Concern of Posterity, oblige me to take Notice of the pernicious Practice of Empiricks of all Orders, with whom it was a Custom to give Emeticks; for certainly many were destroyed by this Practice, the convulsive Reachings to vomit being carried beyond a Possibility to bear it. And truly the best Deliberation and Thought I was able to take in such Exigencies, where I happened to be called, was but of little Effect, and after Administration of the best Medicines that the Rules of Physick could invent, Things generally grew worse; which made it appear as impossible to rectifie a rash and fatal Error in the Conduct of a violent[94] Disease, as in the Management of a military Engagement; but of this we shall have Occasion to say more hereafter.

Y E T to satisfie any inquisitive Person how this primary Affection of the Stomach does arise, and through what Passages the pestilential Poison makes its Entrance, it is to be observed, that nothing is more plain than that the pestilential *Miasmata* not only enter at the larger Passages, but also through the Pores of the Skin, even to the whole nervous System, from whence they are communicated to all other Parts; for this is peculiar to the Nerves, that they not only convey the first Impression to the Stomach by its general Consent with all Parts, but also when that is after any Manner whatsoever affected, they communicate it to the whole Frame, as in the taking a Vomit.

S O M E T I M E S the pestilential *Aura* is mixed with the Food, and swallowed therewith, which after some Delay in the Stomach being digested and dissolved, lets out the imprisoned Venom to vellicate the Fibres into Reachings and convulsive Motions: And to put this altogether out of[95] Dispute, I have often observed Persons immediately to fall sick from a State of perfect Health after eating, and to throw up their Food, in other Respects good and wholsome, as somewhat corrupted and poisonous.

VOMITING also may be promoted by Scents, as well those which are fetid, as such as are contrary, by some particular Antipathy to the Nature and Constitution of the Patient; and this I conjecture happens from the Harmony and Consent of the Organs of Smelling with the Coats of the Stomach, insomuch that the Stomach immediately perceives any Thing that ungratefully strikes the Nose, and rises up against it. In the mean Time I would however transiently make this one Remark, that as in many Cases the Administration of Emeticks was pernicious, whether or no Evacuation of the first Putrefaction at Stomach, might not be much better encouraged upwards by Scents; as, on the contrary, the Reachings at Stomach are sometimes allayed by like Means, as by the Smell of Vinegar, &c. I do confess, that this is a Practice I cannot attest the Success of by[96] Experience, yet it is not unworthy a rational Physician to attempt it.

ALL the Sick likewise quickly after Seizure grew delirious, running wildly about the Streets, if they were not confined by Force; when some tired with Rambling, on Increase of the Distemper, would fall down, ignorant of their Condition, or where they were; and lastly, to repeat what hath been already remarked, that sad Calamity seemed to have complicated in its Production every Thing of a poisonous and a destroying Nature.

MANY were seized with a *Vertigo*, which, without any Motion of external Objects, made them believe their Heads to turn round: Without doubt the Brain grievously suffered from the pestilential Taint, not only because the Spirits used to be clouded, but that all Things were done as if in Sleep, which might arise from the inflammatory, caustick, and narcotick Nature of the Venom, and the Texture and Consent of the Vessels with the various Dispositions of the Fluids. This vertiginous Disposition also in my Opinion[97] might sometimes arise from the inordinate and anomolous Motions of the Spirits.

A great many likewise much complained of the Head-ach, which was so vehement, as if the Parts would have flown asunder; a Complaint the most intolerable of all, because it continued without any Remission or Intervals; the Enemy never retreating of it self, and only to be vanquished by the Efforts of the Constitution, and apposite Medicines. Indeed nothing was more plain, than that the *Meninges* were stimulated by the saline *Spicula* of the Contagion; and from the Inflammation of the Brain, and its Sphacelation in those who died, there is a strong Suspicion that this cruel, shooting Pain continued to the last.

IN this Class of Symptoms, Stupefaction is also to be ranked; because from the Moment of Seizure many were taken with a *Coma*, and slept as if they were dozed with an Opiate; many in the middle of their Employ, with their Friends in Conversation, or other Engagements, (as was before taken notice of) would suddenly,[98] without any Reluctance, fall into profound, and often deadly Sleeps.

BUT by what Means this Venom does exert its narcotick Qualities, is not with me so ready to be accounted for; that is to say, whether it be from its original *Seminium*? Or from Its affinity and Complication with the Scurvy? Or from its predominant Malignity, and Antipathy? Or from an Obstruction of Circulation, or Coagulation, or Extravasation of Blood? Or lastly, from some particular Impression made upon the Origin of the Nerves? For this is a Difficulty reserved for another *Hippocrates*. In the mean while it is by all confessed, that by such Stupefaction or Sleeping, the pestilential Venom becomes not only more deeply rooted, but also more cruelly affects the nervous System, and greatly weakens it.

THE first and most considerable Symptom of the second Class, is a Fever, which (as was before said) was a constant Attendant upon the last Pestilence; although indeed the Infection seemed to kill some before the Blood and other Juices could rise into Fermentation; wherefore it may[99] be taken for granted, that most Persons were accompanied with a Fever. But this Fever indeed was in some very low and concealed, though in others it appeared openly; and he must be but little acquainted in physical Practice, who hath not frequently observed, that in malignant Fevers their Beginnings are hardly discernable, being accompanied with no Heat, no Inequality of Pulse, and no Thirst, although secretly indicated by some other lurking Symptoms; and the Manner in which such Patients expire, demonstrates, that they could not be altogether free of a Fever. There are many Circumstances indeed which make it thus difficult in the Accession to discern its

Approaches, as a Want of Turgescency of Blood in the Veins and Arteries, through Defect of Room for such Commotion and Depuration, or because the Blood is so thin, crude, and degenerate, that it cannot but with Difficulty ferment and grow hot; or because the pestilential *Miasmata* seem at their first Insinuation so friendly to the Constitution, as to stir up no remarkable Alteration in the Blood; or from its cold and styptick Quality, retarding or suppressing such an Agitation.

WHEREFORE no Body should conjecture, that there is no Fever at all, where its manifest Symptoms do not immediately appear; but it most commonly happened otherwise during the late Contagion, for that discovered Signs apparent enough of its Presence, such as extream Inquietude, a most intense Heat outwardly, attended with unquenchable Thirst within, Dryness, Blackness of the Tongue, intolerable Heat of the *Præcordia*, and all other usual Concomitants of a Fever's Accession.

AS to the Fever's Exacerbations and Remissions, it appeared by constant Experience, that sometimes they were erratick and changeable, and at others continued, without any Intervals; and it was also customary to meet with some that wholly remitted for 8, 10, or 12 Hours. The Alternations likewise of Heat and Cold were very various, and with some would change several Times in one Hour, and with others the Periods would be at much greater Distances; so also the recurring Accessions were sometimes milder, and at others more severe. Those who with great Difficulty went through the first Paroxysm,[101] could bear the second with Ease, as being much milder; whereas again the third or fourth Accession would be with intolerable Vehemence and Fury: And at other Times the first Fit would be gentle, and the subsequent very severe and intense; and truly such was the Uncertainty and Disguise of this insidious Enemy, that nothing could be prognosticated of its Attacks or Cruelty.

BUT to come at some tolerable Notion of the Reason for such Uncertainty; it is to be enquired,

FIRST, What Cause can be assigned for such an uncertain Return of the Paroxysms? And,

SECONDLY, What Reason can be given for the unequal Exacerbations when the Fits do recur?

CAN any one doubt what Tumults and Disorders may be excited in the Blood, and other animal Juices, by that saline *Seminium* of a Pestilence, which we have already described? The Uncertainty then of such Disorders must regard either the morbifick Venom, or the Nature and Motion[102] of the Fluids upon which it operates: The morbifick Venom, in Proportion to its Energy, and Disagreement in Figure, irritates Nature, always ready in her own Preservation to expel the Enemy; but when her Exertions are slow, or imperfect, or quite languid, such a Depuration is not obtained; but upon a Remission of the Conflict, there is Space given for interval; and this indeed happens, when the Nature and peculiar Figures of the noxious Particles are such, as may in the first Struggle be broke and subdued, but after some Truce insinuates its Virulence further into the Habit, and imprints upon every Part the true Characteristicks of a fatal Pestilence.

BUT to subdue and throw out the Enemy, the Spirits are at continual Strife, although their Efforts are not always successful; to dispatch this Matter therefore in one Word, as the Assimilation and perfect Mixture of the heterogeneous Particles procures a Motion regular and conformable to the Blood, so from an Inequality and disproportionate Mixture, arises an irregular Circulation and Fermentation, so that the Reason for that Uncertainty in these Fevers, and their irregular Returns[103] and Exacerbations, is to be fought for in the Fluids and their circulating Vessels, and not from any Corruption, or Degree of Putrefaction, according to the Opinion of the Ancients.

AND as for my own Part, I can affirm, that I never could in any one single Instance amongst the infected, find the least Impressions of Corruption in the Blood; and this even those Empiricks, though unwillingly, confess, who, to the vast Detriment of the Sick, let them Blood upon such a Notion; none of them having been ever able to discover any Signs of Corruption in their Blood, which as conscious of it self blushed for their fatal Mistake, and in this Distemper commonly appeared more florid than at other Times.

THAT the Times of the Paroxysms should be uncertain, I take owing to the Inability of the Constitution to struggle with the pestilential Venom; for as every Fever is accounted regular, where all its Changes are uniform and distinct, by Reason of the managable and ductile Disposition of the morbifick Matter; so, on the contrary, where the pestilential *Miasmata*[104] uncertainly exert themselves, and excite new Commotions, either by the Obstinacy or Asperity of their Parts not yielding to Comminution, there a Fever returns with inconstant and unexpected Exacerbations: But to hasten to the subsequent Symptoms.

ALTHOUGH some (as before said) were buried in Sleep, yet others suffered by a very different Extream, and kept continually waking, insomuch that frequent Repetitions of the most efficacious Opiates could not procure the least Composure; in which Case, it is my Opinion, that the Membranes of the Brain are pricked and vellicated by poisonous *Spicula*; besides which also those soft, dewy Moistures upon the Brain, necessary for its Relaxation to sleep, are dissipated and exhaled by the burning Heat of the Fever; so that the Spirits are, as it were, set on Fire, and Inflammations raised, not to be again extinguished, and frequently likewise Sphacelations of the Brain.

BUT the most remarkable Symptoms of this Class, is the Palpitation of the Heart, the Ancients conjectur'd that Pestilential *Aura* to have a specifick Contrariety to[105] the Nature of that Organ; and it must be confessed that in the late Sickness this Complaint was very grievous; but yet I cannot see how this Venom should more particularly be pointed against the Heart than any other of the *Viscera*, unless in Consideration to the greater Importance of its Office in the OEconomy.

As soon as the subtile Poison of a Contagion hath insinuated it self into the Mass of Blood, either through the Pores of the Skin, or other more open Passages, there is no doubt, but it imprints upon it very malignant Qualities, which, according to the necessary Laws of Circulation, must arrive at the Heart it self, and affect it with Uneasiness, so that its Palpitation is nothing else than its Struggles to throw off what is Offensive; and it is no wonder to me this happens, because the Heart is composed of such a Contexture of Fibres; for as the Pestilential Venom hath somewhat in it of a saline Nature, and what is acrid, it very naturally stimulates the nervous Parts, and gives to this Organ even convulsive Motions; but of this matter every one hath leave to judge for himself.

[106]

BUT how vehemently the Heart may beat on this Occasion, appears very manifest from a remarkable Instance; I was sent for to a Youth of about fourteen Years of Age, who had continued free of the Infection, after his Mother and the rest of the Family had been visited by it, when all on a sudden he was seized with such a Palpitation at Heart, That I and several others could hear it at some considerable Distance, and it continued so to do till he died, which was soon after; many Medicines being given without any manner of Success: But in so extraordinary a Case as this, I am apt to conjecture it rather owing to a Pestilential Carbuncle seizing the Heart it self, than from the Vellication and *Stimulus* only of pungent Particles passing through it.

BUT to go on in the Enumeration of Symptoms, Sweat deserves mention, because sometimes it breaks out in such Profusion as if the whole Constitution was dissolved, and with a vast Loss of Spirits and Strength, to the imminent Danger of the Patient, by such a Dissipation of Spirits, such a Colliquation of the Balsam[107] of Life, and an Extinction of the natural Heat. And indeed I know nothing that more powerfully attenuates the Humours, and more suddenly puts all the animal Juices into Fusion, so as to run them through the Pores of the Skin, and the pestilential nitro-aereal Poyson; and by whose colliquative Quality even the fleshy Parts are dissolved and exhaled in vapour.

THESE Sweats also of the Infected are not only profuse, but also variously coloured; in some of a citron Hue, in others Purple, in some green or black, and in others like Blood; which I take to be from the various Dispositions of the morbifick Venom, to give different Tinctures to the Humours: And by this Means some experienced Nurses could prognosticate the Event of the Distemper from the Colour of the Cloaths or Linen tinged with the Sweat.

THE Sweat of some would be so fetid and intolerable, from a kind of Empyreumatick Disposition, possibly, of the Juices, that no one could endure his Nose within the Stench; sometimes it was sharp, and in a Manner caustick; and hence it 108 was easy to judge from what Origin the Pestilence derived its Qualities, *viz.* From a sharp and burning *Ichor*, that would even excoriate the Parts, and sometimes vesicate them, as if scalding Water had been poured upon them.

SOMETIMES cold Sweats would break out, while the Heat raged inwardly, and excited unquenchable Drought. Some continued in a Profusion of Sweat until Life it self exhaled with it, while others had short Intervals of Truce and Cessation; nay, some at the same time sweat on one Side, while the other was quite parched with Dryness.

BUT the Benefit of this Evacuation, when it was regular, either natural or by Art, was so manifest, that all the Infected that recovered were sensible of it, and greatly rejoyced at its good Effects; for those pestilential Particles, which eluded the Power of all other Means, immediately upon a Sweat, as at a common Signal, made their Escape with the transpiring Steam; but whensoever Diaphoreticks could not conquer the Coagulation, Viscidity, or Obstinacy of the pestilential Poyson, 109 it always went very bad, being commonly followed by a Symptomatical Sweat, and a fatal Separation of the animal Fluids.

YET the Energy of the pestilential Contagion not only freely discovered its self in these Profusions amongst the Living, who (as already observed) were dissolved as in an *Helodes* and a *Typhodes*, but commonly the very Carcases when dead, would weep out, as it were, the morbid Ferment, both through the cutaneous Pores, and the common lachrymal Ducts of the Eyes.

THERE is no Occasion to say much concerning Hemorrhages at Nose; this Symptom happening much more often from the Colliquative Nature of the Poison, and its Erosion of the Vessels, than from a Plethora; as is evident more from the ichorous Colour of the Blood than its continual Distillation from those Vessels.

Were it not here that we study all possible Brevity, many other Symptoms might be enumerated which commonly attended this pestilential Fever, as Heat of 110 the *Præcordia*, Hiccup, Gripings, *&c.* all which I at present pass by, and close the whole with such as are more peculiar to it, particularly those poisonous Vesications commonly called *Blains*.

THESE Vesications used commonly to rise with an exquisite and shooting Pain, containing a serous Humour or *Ichor*, for the most part of a Yellowish or Straw Colour, and encompassed with a variegated Circle, generally Reddish.

THESE Pustules broke out in many Parts of the Body; and as their Station was various, so their Number was also uncertain; in some they were few, in others many, and a Woman I once met with covered all over with them; as to their Bigness, they were also uncertain; for some were as a small Pea, while others increased to the Magnitude of a Nutmeg.

THE included Matter (near perhaps to the Nature of Urine) was altogether incapable of Suppuration, as it was saline and almost caustick; for very soon after its Eruption it would corrode its Vesicle, and 111 burst out, of a Colour yellowish, livid, or black. Moreover, the surrounding Circle was not always of the same Appearance, although at first coming out it was continually inflamed.

BUT this is highly observable, that sometimes these Vesicles broke out without any other previous Indications of Infection, and, as I imagine, from the expeditious Separation of the pestilential Venom, and the sudden Conquest of the Distemper by a strong Constitution: But whensoever the Pain and Heat of the Part was so aggravated, that no proper Applications would asswage it, there was commonly Danger of a Mortification from so great a Concourse of pestilential Particles together; and once I remember a Vesicle to change into a Carbuncle, from the continued Accession to it of fresh morbifick Poison.

WE come now in Course to speak of Buboes, which were hard and painful Tumours, with Inflammation and Gathering upon the Glands, behind the Ears, Arm-Pits, or Groin.

112

THESE Tumors immediately upon Seizure are found so hard, that they will not at all give Way to the Touch. In some these were moveable, and in others fixed; but after some Time this great Tension remitted; and it was common to prognosticate the Event of

27

the Distemper from their sudden or slow Increase, and from their genuine or untoward Suppuration, as also from the Degrees of Virulence in their Contents.

THE Groans and unfeigned Tears of the Sick too plainly expressed the Aggravations of their Miseries, and some seemed even to drown their Sense of Pain with their Complainings; and this Intenseness of Pain cannot be a Wonder to any, who duly consider either the Nature of the pestilential Venom, or the Constitution of the Glands. I have already so largely discoursed of the Virulence and corrosive Qualities of the pestilential Poison, that no more need here be said about it; and whosoever examines the Glands will find, that from the great Distention of the Vessels, in this Case, the Buboes must chiefly owe their Rise to a Correspondence between the Nerves and Lymphaticks, and the Juices they contain.

MANY Persons of publick Note have elegantly given the Anatomy and Use of the Glands; it is therefore sufficient for my Purpose here to shew, how from an Obstruction of those Juices, which flow through the larger Nerves, particularly of the Arms and Thighs, and their subservient Vessels, and their Impregnation with heterogeneous and poisonous Particles, Buboes do arise.

IF any one makes it a Doubt, why these Tumors should rather come in the above-mentioned Places, rather than on the *parotide*Glands, let such consider, that it is owing to the Magnitude and Capacity of the Nerves and Vessels constituting the Glands of those Parts; as also that their different Dispositions to Suppuration does proceed from the same Cause.

BUT that this Affair may more fully appear, it is to be discovered from what Source that Matter flows, which degenerates into Matter, and discharges from a Buboe in so great Plenty.

IN the Prosecution of this Enquiry, it shall not be without a Colour, at least, of Reason, that I shall dissent from an Opinion both of Ancients and Moderns, about the Blood alone being immediately changed into Matter; for I rather think it to proceed from other Juices; and this I shall endeavour to support by the following Arguments.

AND first of all, notwithstanding the Blood which runs in the Arteries and Veins does sometimes, though very seldom, appear whitish; it then happens from too great a Mixture either of nutritious Juice, or of a degenerate Chyle, that will not easily change, and take its red Colour; but it never passes into Matter, because the necessary Conditions of Circulation will not admit of so much Rest as is requisite thereunto; besides, even the extravasated Blood will not easily undergoe such an Alteration: For when any Vessels, and chiefly the Capillaries, are so obstructed by Contusions, or any other Means, that the neighbouring Parts swell, every Physician and Surgeon too, I hope, knows that discutient Medicines and Cataplasms will restore the former Motion and Fluxity to the Blood, ease the Pain, and dissipate the Tumour.

IF the Blood be too fluid in the Arteries, it is apt to occasion *Anaeurisms*, and in the capillary Veins an *Ecchymosis*; but nothing is more commonly observed in Practice, that upon a Recovery of the Blood's due Constitution and Circulation, the obstructed Matter in an*Ecchymosis* will dissipate through the Pores of the Skin, or be absorbed by the refluent Blood: But when the Blood happens to be too grumous and stagnate, a Fever immediately arises, unless it be prevented by Evacuation; and in such a Disorder every one knows that there is most Danger of a *Schirrus*, or a Mortification.

AND as it hath been already observed that Blood could not be drawn from the infected by Phlebotomy, without Loss of Strength, if not of Life, whereas the greater Quantities of *Pus* were obtained by Suppuration of their Buboes, the Patient was so much the better for it; it seems consonant to Reason, that if *Pus* was generated immediately from the Blood, the Strength would as much decay upon its Loss, as upon Phlebotomy: But I have always found it, (as many Times already observed) that how little soever the Quantity of Blood drawn away was, and although done at several Times, yet it proved of more Prejudice to the Patient than an hundred times as much Matter drawn from a Buboe; and that the whole remaining Mass was not able to recruit the Loss sustained thereby.

IF they who espouse a contrary Opinion, should suggest that Blood may be drawn from a Tumour imperfectly suppurated, and from thence conclude, that its Origin was from the Arterial and Venal Fluids; it may be readily answered, that on opening a fresh Tumour, a bloody *Ichor* will flow out, because in the Operation some Blood-Vessels will be cut; whereas when the Tumour is in Maturation, the Quantity of Humour there collected obstructs the Blood from flowing to it through its proper Vessels; and which Humour, altho' in it self at first more thin and crude, yet by the Heat of its neighbouring Parts, and its own natural Disposition, it will afterwards thicken, and change into a white Colour of a laudable Consistence.

T H I R D L Y, To the foregoing it may be added, that so far as the Blood partakes of a saline Quality, by so much the less will it be disposed to change into Matter; for the same Reason that Sea-Water cannot be boiled into a Gelly; for Salt adds to the Fluxility of Fluids, and thereby prevents Incrassation, unless in those Instances where they of themselves chrystallize, by Means of an Incapacity of the *Menstruum* to keep them in Solution, which is foreign to the Case before us.

L A S T L Y, Nothing is more known in Nature, than that Blood, by what Means soever extravasated, if it cannot get back again into the Vessels, will, after some Stagnation, run for the most Part into Grume; so that when a Fluctuation requires opening, little else than a coagulated Blood flows out: And if any one please to receive the Blood from an opened Vein into a warm Porringer, and afterwards place it in a luted Vessel upon a Sand Heat, as near as possible equal to that which is natural, he will find all Labour lost in endeavouring to produce thereby any Appearances of *Pus* in it, either from its Colour, Smell, or any other of its requisite Properties.

W H Y then may we not conclude with some others of great Note, that *Pus* is generated immediately from the nutritious Juice, not in the Arteries and Veins, but in other Vessels; in which Juice all the requisite Properties are to be found, as a Disposition to grow thick, without Smell, white, light, and of a smooth Consistence; and I take it to be very probable, that the *Pus* is made from hence by the Assistance of the natural Heat, and the Conveyance of it by the forementioned Vessels into the Glands whereinto they are complicated, and not by any Means from the Venal Blood, and much less from the Arterial.

B U T least I should seem to digress too far; the *Sanies* thrown out by a Buboe is very different, sometimes thin and ichorous, at others thicker and more laudable, as in Abscesses that are not malignant; in Respect of its Smell, it is sometimes so extreamly fetid, as not to be endured by the Nose; but always the more plentifully it discharges, the better does the Patient fare afterwards: Nature finds a Vent this open Way to disengage her self from a pernicious Enemy.

T H E Number of Buboes was uncertain, sometimes one only appeared, at others, which was most commonly, two broke out at once; nay, there were met with Instances wherein all the Glands capable of it were tumified. Many Buboes at a Time infallibly demonstrated the Aggravation, and Dispersion of the virulent Taint; and on the contrary, but few shewed the Poison to be not so prevalent, more contracted, and brought to a narrower Compass for Expulsion.

The Places, and Manner of their Eruption was very uncertain, sometimes one would appear in the right *Axilla*, and another on the contrary Side of the Groin; these Tumours would likewise sometimes last but a Day, and again insensibly vanish, that is, always when profuse Sweat arose; but whensoever they were drawn in again by any Mismanagement or Casualty, they would appear and vanish again many Times, and be very difficult afterwards to be fixed; and sometimes when they could be brought to Suppuration, and a plentiful Discharge, they would renew again, as we shall hereafter have further Occasion to observe.

T H E Parotides borrow their Names from the Glands affected, which grow behind the Ears; but these Tumours are not to be distinguished from others but by their Situation, and therefore require not any particular Description here, so that amongst many Instances I shall give but one to discover their Nature; In a certain Youth there arose a *Parotis* on each Side, behind the Ears, which after Suppuration and Incision, let out great Quantities of *Pus*, and were afterwards by a Surgeon healed up; but the musculous Flesh was at this Time so wasted, as to discover a Sight as pleasant as strange, *viz.* the external jugular Veins, with the Arteries under them, the recurrent Nerves, the Tendons, the OEsophagus, and in short all the Vessels quite bare and untouched; but upon the Patient's Recovery all filled up as before with new Flesh.

A Conjecture of *Diemebrooeck* comes here in our Way to examine; he will have it that Buboes are produced from an Ebullition[121] of a saline and an acid Humour meeting together, like a Mixture of Salt of Tartar and Spirit of Vitriol: But whence can such a vast Coagulation arise? Indeed I do not deny but that a Tumult and Bustle may be occasioned by the Concourse of such Principles, as also that from such a Collucatation some saline Particles may be precipitated; and it must further be allowed, that a Part will inflate and swell while such Fermentation continues; but yet I cannot apprehend how *Pus* can be generated by such Means; for by an Effusion of such a Mixture the *Serum* would be more changed into a *Lixivium*, than a purulent Matter; after the Conflict likewise is over, the Tumour would immediately subside and vanish; but, on the contrary, Buboes daily and gradually come to their Height of Suppuration: But I shall not detain the Reader on this Head any longer, but proceed to a Description of a Carbuncle.

A Carbuncle then is a small Eruption, whose Contents are soon discharged, after which it appears in a crusty Tubercle about the Bigness of a Millet Seed, gradually spreading, and encompassed with a very red[122]and fiery Circle; arising first of all from an ichorous Humour, afterwards with great Pain and Heat, from a lixivious and caustick Poison.

THAT I may dispatch as much as possible in a few Words, it now lies before me to describe the common Method of its Eruption; in the Beginning is a sharp pricking Pain upon the Part affected, which in a little Time grows very hot, and then lifts up the Cuticle into a Blister, containing a thin *Ichor*; but after the Vesicle is by rubbing or any other Accident broke, and the contained Fluid by Heat dissipated, its caustick Quality leaves an *Eschar* behind, which crusts over, in some sooner, and in others later; its Extension is various, sometimes more broad, and at others more contracted; nor is its Colour more certain; in the greatest Degree of Inflammation it is extreamly red, but for the most Part it is dusky, very often livid, and sometimes, from the peculiar Virulence of the pestilential Poison, even quite black.

BUT as there is a Quality in the pestilential Venom not yielding even to an actual Cautery, and from which in the[123] Production of Carbuncles *Eschars* are generated, I take it to be of Consequence to know how such a sharp, burning, and caustick Humour comes to be bred in an humane Body; and by what Contrivance of Nature it comes to be thus separated and thrown out?

AND in an Affair of this Difficulty, I expect to be candidly set right by any one who thinks me mistaken. The whole Tribe of Diseases an humane Constitution is subject to, does undeniably prove that our Bodies are capable of producing many venomous Taints, even equal to any Thing in the Air or the Earth; nay, the Histories of Physick give many Instances of poisonous Insects and Animals bred within us; and no one can be ignorant, that besides the Disposition of corrupted Humours within us to generate such Creatures, that their *Semina* are often brought to us from without: And this is very manifest in a *private*Pestilence, (if that Term may be allowed me) where, without any Help from external Contagion, not only a poisonous *Seminium* may be generated, but Carbuncles also may break out; that is, from the peculiar[124]caustick Quality of saline Particles in the Body.

WHEREFORE if this can be done in a *private* Pestilence, what may we not expect from a Pestilence that is the Consequence of an Epidemick Cause; for the additional Assistance of a more powerful saline Principle from without, cannot but greatly actuate the animal Juices, and induce a compound Malignity abundantly sufficient for the Production of pestilential Carbuncles.

THE more aggravated therefore the saline Qualities of this foreign saline Principles shall be, and in Proportion to the Quantities of it insinuated into the animal Fluids, the Carbuncles will break out more or fewer, sooner or later; although as long as the pestilential Poison flows in Company with other Fluids within the Vessels, it seems more mild, because then diluted, than when separated and thrown upon the Skin by the natural Excretory Powers. And this Expulsion of it seems much to be assisted by the common Tendency of serous Particles towards the Surface, and the Congress of nitro-aereal[125] Particles therewith; but nothing however is more manifest than that when the pestilential Poison hath got to the

Surface, it exercises its Virulence upon all the Parts it touches, and leaves cruel Marks of its Triumph behind; the same as which likewise obtains not only from an epidemick Pestilence, but upon drinking any poisonous Draughts.

BUT it concerns us here to remove one Mistake; For it is laid down by *Diemebrooeck*, in Opposition to the common Opinion, that a Carbuncle is nothing else but an actual Gangrene; for if any Credit may be given to our Experience, which we look upon to be as well founded as that of this great Man, I do not remember any Carbuncles (unless where there hath some manifest Error been committed in external Applications, or the Virulence of the Pestilence hath been greater than ordinary) to have tended more to a Sphacelation, than any other Consequences of the pestilential Poison.

And were there not innumerable Testimonies to the Truth of this, many Arguments might be alledged in its Vindication;[126] for while there is a free Influx of vital Spirits, and other natural Fluids, into the Part affected; while the native Heat is preserved from Suffocation, and Putrefaction is prevented, what Person can imagine there to be any particular Disposition to Mortification in a single Carbuncle? And the more especially when the Spirits are so far from being intercepted by the Carbuncle's Eruption, that they flow more plentifully to the Part; when the native Heat is so far from being suffocated; that by its Assistance a salutary Separation is made; and lastly, when the Part affected is so far from Putrefaction, and rendered more humid than before, that these saline Particles of an escharotick Quality, rather prevent Mortification, and by drying the Part make it rather more able to resist such a Change: And according to the best of my Remembrance, I never did meet with a Carbuncle that mortified, unless from the Mismanagement or Carelesness of Surgeons, or when the highest Degree of Virulence in the pestilential Poison had not occasioned an immediate Sphacelation.

[127]

NO Part of an humane Body was free from the Eruption of the Carbuncles; And I shall not exceed the Truth if I affirm that I have met with them at one time or other in all Places. But this Matter will yet appear more fully beyond Contradiction, when I shall have brought a few select Instances out of a great Multitude, to put it quite out of Dispute.

A Girl of about 12 Years of Age, felt a grievous Pain about her Breast, where quickly after the Appearance of a Pimple, there broke out a Carbuncle; the *Eschar* at last came off, and the Ulcer discharging some Matter plentifully; after about twenty Days she was reckoned to be very well, had not a Surgeon too rashly dressed her with the *red drying Ointment*, in order to cicatrize it; for upon that the Pestilence appeared again, and killed her in about three Days, undoubtedly from a Return of the Venom inwards before it was all discharged.

ANOTHER Case, almost beyond Belief, were it not attested by many Eye-Witnesses, was of a Woman, who immediately[128] after Delivery had a Carbuncle appear upon her Breasts, when the Infant sucked all the Time without Harm, and the Woman, through the Favour of the Season, and exact Care in all Respects, recovered. I was also another time called to a Man of advanced Years, whose whole Thigh and Hip was over-run with a Carbuncle, but the Vesication was made by such an ichorous *Serum*, that I strongly suspected a Mortification; I complained of being called so late, but however ordered a deep Scarification, and other Means suitable, whereupon there grew some Hopes of Separation, but for Want of inward Strength and Spirits, the Patient died; whereas another of a more vigorous Habit, was recovered in the same Case, for no other Reason, but that there was Strength enough to carry him through it. Moreover, I once met with a Buboe and Carbuncle together in the Groin of a Boy, not above two Finger's Breadth of each other; but by due Means, both medicinal and chirurgical, the Lad got well from both his Ails together.

A certain Merchant had a Carbuncle upon his Arm, a little below the Elbow,[129] but what was most unhappy was, that at the Beginning he was so Impatient of the Pain, that he applyed a Cooling Cataplasm to it of his own ordering, for suddenly thereupon it changed into a Gangrene, to obviate which, Scarrification was immediately had recourse to, in the Execution of which, the Surgeon inadvertently cut a large Vein, which caused such a Flux of Blood, as could not be stopped by either actual Cautery, or any other Means; whereupon followed such a Sinking of his Spirits, that the unfortunate Gentleman died in three Hours time.

31

LASTLY, A Carbuncle appeared on the Finger of a young Woman, to eradicate which, we took all imaginable Care; and all Things at first seemed to answer our Wishes; but the Uncertainty of humane Expectations! for the Patient with her old Nurse Supping plentifully upon *French* Beans, that very Night the Distemper returned; and although she vomited as much as her Strength would bear, by the Provocation of an Emetick given her, after which were used the most Cordial Remedies, and the most warm Alexipharmicks, early in the Morning, a fresh Carbuncle came130 in the Place of the old one; she was delirious all that Day, and in the Evening she expired. After the Bearers came that Night to bury her, and talked of fetching away the old Woman next, as a Person dead, the poor Wretch, as awakened from Sleep, cried out, she was not dead; but she disappointed not their Agreement, and died time enough to be carried away the same Night to the burying Place.

I might easily imploy a Volume in a Recital of all the particular Circumstances of these Carbuncles; but however, before I dismiss this Subject, I cannot omit that the pestilential Venom was in a very great Manner communicable from one Carbuncle to another; or to speak perhaps more properly, the saline Virulence of a Carbuncle would generate another wheresoever it lodged.

THE Number of Carbuncles was undeterminate, sometimes two, three, four, or more, would come out at once, the pestilential Venom being diffused to many Parts at the same Time; but the rest we shall leave to that Section concerning the Cure of Carbuncles; we shall here therefore subjoin131 somewhat concerning pestilential Spots, called *Petechiæ*.

THE Petechiæ then are little Spots upon the Skin, not easily distinguishable from a Flea-Bite; though this Difference may be observed, in a Flea-Bite there may be seen a Puncture in the middle, where the little Creature had struck in its Teeth, and round it an Inflammation, with a little extravasated Blood: But these Spots are more uniform in their Colour, more fixed, and difficult to be removed, whereas upon any Pressure with the Finger a Flea-Bite gives Way, except in the central Puncture. Furthermore the pestilential *Petechiæ* are to be distinguished from the Spots of a malignant Fever, as they are deeper coloured; and likewise to be known (as before observed) from Scurvy Spots, which are much broader, and not always exactly round; although these are likewise sometimes intermixed with the pestilential ones, and by Means of the aforementioned Affinities between them, hardly in some Cases to be distinguished.

TO this it may be added, that the pestilential *Petechiæ* do not always fix in the132 same Parts, and sometimes they disappear, after a short Stay in one Place, and immediately rise in others: And indeed there is no Part altogether exempted from them, although they chiefly come out in the Neck, Breast, and Back; whereas those of the Scurvy come mostly in the extream Parts. The Reason of this in the former Case may probably be from the Proximity of the larger Vessels, and the Largeness of the Pores about the Trunk of the Body; and in the Scurvy, the Legs particularly are most spotted, from the Tendency and Precipitation of the saline Particles downwards.

THE Spots were sometimes few, but most commonly very numerous; in some they were so thick, as to cover in a manner the whole Skin. I saw a little Girl that was all over full with them, but upon a large Sweat arising, they all disappeared, and she recovered; yet sometimes the Distemper was so delusory, that these Spots would arise, and disappear, and come out again, for several Times; that is, when Nature gave its utmost Efforts to expel the Poison, they might be seen upon the Surface; but when the Spirits languished,133 or upon any external Cold, they would go in again.

I might here conveniently observe, that this Eruption was almost always symptomatical, and very rarely critical; the Colour of them was not always the same, sometimes they were red, or purple, at others yellow, and sometimes livid or black, according to the Nature and Energy of the morbifick Venom, and its Complication with other Contingencies; and hence we naturally pass to the essential Characteristicks of a Pestilence.

THE genuine pestilential Characters, by the common People amongst us called *Tokens*, as the Pledges or Fore-warnings of Death, are nothing else than minute and distinct *Blasts*, which have their Origin from within, and rise up with a little pyramidal Protuberance, having the pestilential Poison chiefly collected at their Bases, and, according to the accustomed Dispersion of such Agents, gradually tainting the neighbouring Parts, and reaching to the Surface, as the Configuration of Vessels and Pores are disposed to favour their Spreading.

134

MOREOVER these Blasts were derivable from external Causes, as from the Injuries of Air, where the pestilential *Miasmata* were pent up and condensed, and by that Means their Virulence increased to that Degree, that Life it self was immediately extinguished, upon coming within their Reach. Nay, some were so suddenly marked with these fatal Characters, that they did not before find themselves in any other Respect out of Order; which is a Circumstance so well known, that there is little need to confirm it by particular Instances, however, for the Reader's Satisfaction, I shall recollect one or two Facts of this Kind.

I was called to a Girl the first Day of her Seizure, who breathed without any Difficulty, her Warmth was moderate and natural, her Inwards free from glowing and Pain, and her Pulse not unequal or irregular; but, on the contrary, all Things genuine and well, as if she had ailed nothing; and indeed I was rather inclined to think she counterfeited being sick, than really to be out of Order, until examining her Breast, I found the certain Characters135 of Death imprinted in many Places; and in that following Night she died, before she her self, or any Person about her, could discern her otherwise out of Order.

Some time after I visited a Widow of Sixty Years of Age, whom I met with at Dinner, where she had eat heartily of Mutton, and filled besides her Stomach with Broth; after I had enquired into several Particulars relating to her Health, she affirmed her self to have never been better in her Life, but upon feeling her Pulse, I perceived it to intermit, and upon examining her Breast, I found an Abundance of Tokens, which proved too true a Prognostick, that even after so good a Dinner she would by the Evening be in another World.

AS to the Eruption of these fatal Characters, I judged them to be rather the Effects of the pestilential corrosive Salt, than of any Putrefaction of the Humours; for this Poison wanting room for Exhalation through the Pores of the Skin, collected in Quantities upon the Surface, and for want of Spirits to strive therewith, imprinted these Marks thereupon.

136

FURTHERMORE these external Parts not only grew dry from the Acrimony of this Venom, but were also very liable to Sphacelation by an Extinction of the vital Spirits; but enough of this, because it would be but adding Light to the Noon-day Sun, to endeavour to confirm it by more Testimonies.

THESE Tokens did differ in Regard to their Colour and Hardness; of their Colour we shall speak hereafter: Their Hardness I used to try with a Needle or Penknife, to see whether the Sense and Life was perished or not; in which Trials I found a great deal of Difference, as some would be penetrated with very little Trouble, when others were even callous and horny, and difficult to be penetrated. The Origin of these I conjecture to be from the nervous Juice, or some gelatinous Substance evaporated into a gummy Consistence, not unlike those horny Excrescencies from the Bones; their Colour and Affinity in many Respects with Wharts is also remarkable.

137

AND here I cannot pass by an Instance worth Observation, of a Girl who came to my House full of Sadness and Consternation, already even to sink down; upon Examination she told me that she had broke out from an House where she was shut up with a Nurse, all the rest of the Family being dead, to shew me the certain Forerunner of Death upon her, saying she had the *Tokens* upon her Leg; but I soon found a Mistake that might have been fatal to her, for it was only a Whart, which neither she nor the Nurse had ever taken Notice of before; she was soon undeceiv'd, and by my Encouragement shook off all her Fear; returning Home chearful to take those Medicines which were directed to carry off the Disorders upon her, and sweating her plentifully removed all Suspicion of the Contagion: But I really believe, that had not her Mind been soon made easie, by what was said to her, she would have died merely by the Force of her Imagination; as such a Dread extreamly aggravates the least Complaints.

BUT some of these *Tokens* were not only so like in Appearance to Wharts, that138 they deceived this young Girl, for sometimes even the Surgeons mistook them; and I was beholden to the Management beforementioned of pricking through them to be satisfied sometimes my self, as well as to know the Degrees of Malignity in the Venom of the true *Tokens*; where I found quickly a Sensibility, I took it for a good Sign, and those which went no further than the Skin, would oftentimes slough off; whereas when they went deeper, they were deemed dangerous, especially when the Part lost its Feeling, and threatned Sphacelation. There were likewise some found so extreamly comatous, that the whole Body was deprived of Sense; insomuch that if any Limb, or Part clear of the *Tokens*, was tried by Puncture, or Incision, there would be no more felt than upon the deadly Marks themselves; notwithstanding which Insensibility of Body, some Faculties of the Mind would return and be perceived even till Death.

THE Viscera also, as well as the external Parts, would sometimes be marked with these Characters, nay, sometimes it appeared, that the Inwards were affected,139 when nothing of the *Tokens* were seen externally.

THE Magnitude of the *Tokens* were various, sometimes as small as a Pin's Head, and at others larger, and as broad as a Silver Peny; there were indeed Instances of many running into one, but this was but seldom in the late Sickness.

LASTLY, Some were depressed, and others prominent, and some did not appear till the infected Person was dead; so that it did not suffice to kill, but also to leave Marks of its Triumph; but some of the crafty Nurses would put the dead Body immediately into wet Cloaths, whereby they stopped the further Fermentation of the Juices, and restrained such Eruption, in Order to elude the Magistrates Notice and Power, to shut up the Houses.

BUT how much soever these deep Marks were the sure Fore-warnings of Death, yet sometimes they would be out from the fourth Day before, and remain all that while as terrible Admonitions both to the Sick and others.

140

SECTION VI.

The Prognostick Signs of the late Pestilence.

AS that Pestilence which of late made so great Havock amongst Mankind, was so full of Shiftings and Changes in its Attacks and Progress, that very little Certainty could be had of its Event; it highly concerns the Credit and Honour of the Faculty, not too hastily in such Cases to prognosticate either Recovery or Death: In Order therefore to remove, as much as possible, such Difficulties for the future, it is with Cheerfulness that I can leave with Posterity those Observations which I have been able to make in my daily Attendance upon the Infected, to the utmost Hazard of my Life, through the Course of this late Sickness.

THE prognostick Signs then regard either the Pestilence it self, as to its Origin, Heighth, and Declension, or the Recovery or Death of the Patient.

141

FROM certain and undoubted Signs, for some time foregoing the manifest Eruption of the Plague, may its Degrees of Severity be prognosticated.

AS sharp and immoderate Pains apparently denote a pestilential Constitution, and likewise Tumours breaking out again upon Parts before affected: For it is a Case that I have often met with, that those who have had Buboes and Carbuncles in the Sickness well cured, to break out again afterwards, from some Remains of the pestilential Venom yet lurking in the Constitution, and not to be conquered.

WHENSOEVER chronick Diseases are changed into acute ones, it may be concluded that the Infection is not far off; For Valetudinarians are more sensible of any approaching Disorder than those who are strong and healthful: And from a natural Cause may it be accounted why infirm Constitutions can certainly foretel several Changes in the Air, and be forewarn'd of other external Inconveniencies; and the more virulent any Infectious *Miasmata* are, the sooner do they affect such Habits;142 and it seems peculiar to the Plague to be preceded by its pernicious *Effluvia*, like so many Officers seizing the Weak and Helpless first; and such it tyrannizes over by converting the morbid Humours into its own Nature, in subtilizing those which are gross, acuating the dull, heating the cold, changing the natural Ferments, and in short, by inducing opposite Qualities into the whole Constitution.

MOREOVER, in this Regard we may consider the frequent Mortalities amongst Cattle, which foregoe an Infection amongst Mankind; for these Creatures living for the most Part, both Night and Day, in the open Air, not only are more influenced by it when tainted, but are also hurt by the infectious Venom which gathers upon the Herbage; as likewise they are more liable, on other Accounts, to feel its first Approaches, because its freest Progress is in open Places.

MOREOVER, when there is a general Sadness and Consternation upon the Minds of the People from no manifest Cause, so that the whole Multitude are pale and spiritless, who can think but[143] that some general Calamity is at Hand?

AND certainly this will not appear a very difficult Conjecture, and remote from Reason, when we duly consider the strange Intercourse and Familiarity which the Spirits maintain with Things very occult, and at a Distance; for whosoever rightly weighs this Matter, will perceive the Spirits capable of very subtle Impressions, by Means of their Intercourses with the Imagination, whereby they are capable of perceiving, though obscurely, any approaching Evil, and consequently of exciting amongst the Populace a general Apprehension concerning Futurity, without any miraculous Influence.

LASTLY, All fore-bodings of any Kind denote the Malignancy of the approaching Evil, because they are manifestly from the Influence of the pestilential *Miasmata*; and the further off such Impressions are made, the greater do they prognosticate the future Calamity will be; because such Irradiations at a Distance, and propagated through a long Tract of Air, denote the great Energy and Virulence of their Origin; when therefore the Pestilence[144] seldom appears without such Fore-warnings, and gradually diffuses according to the greater or lesser Liberty for the nitro-aerial Poison to move in, and the first Perceptions of it are so terrible, what Miseries and Desolations may not be expected from it, when it is arrived in its full Force?

A Pestilence that is fierce and deadly in its first Attack, soon ceases.

I call such a Pestilence fierce, that immediately destroys the strongest Constitutions, and which being every where diffused, seizes all at once; for the sooner the venomous *Seminium* is spread and wasted, the sooner will its Fury be over.

THE Times of a Pestilence in its Decrease, are in Proportion to the Times of its Increase.

FOR the infectious Poison does not act precariously, but in a regular and uniform Manner, as it fully appeared by the Course of the late Sickness amongst us; (not to mention others at a greater Distance of Place and Time) but this will be best[145] made appear from the Tables of Mortality hereunto annexed.

The Cause of a Pestilence being removed, spent, or extinguished, its Effects immediately cease.

AS Fire goes out when its Fuel is wanting, or spent, so the pestilential Virulence continually wants somewhat to keep it up, and no longer than it is supplied with that necessary *Pabulum* will it last: Although I acknowledge that sometimes these fatal Sparks will lie as it were smothered in their own Ruins, for some Time, and after a certain Interval break out again into its first Fury, from the original Cause that as yet hath never been extinguished. And hence perhaps some may be led into an Error about the Plague's being co-æval with the World, and its continual Subsistance in one Place or another, as external Circumstances favour its Propagation or Hindrance; for the very Increase of the pestilential *Seminium*, after every Interval of Recess, plainly shews it to take fresh Root; and upon the total Extirpation of it, I cannot see how the same can appear again:[146] And this is confirmed by the almost continual Varieties in different Infections.

WE now come in Course to speak of those Prognosticks, which regard the Death or Recovery of the infected.

Every Hemorrhage is bad, but a Flux of the Menses always fatal.

A Looseness of the Bowels, especially in the Beginning, is commonly a Sign of Death.

BECAUSE by this Evacuation a *Diaphoresis* is prevented, the Strength is wasted, and the Poison is so far thrown upon the Bowels, as sometimes to induce Sphacelation; the

Case if likewise not much better when the *Fæces* are extreamly fetid, and there is no Relief thereby; or when they are green, or black, or come away involuntarily, especially when attended with a *Dysentery*.

WHERE the Lungs are tender, weak, or distempered, it generally ends ill.

FOR I can hardly remember any one who had bad Lungs that escaped in the late Sickness; and it was a constant Observation, that Asthmatick Persons, not only by frequent and hard Inspiration drew in more of the poysonous Steams than others, but also that the weakned Force of that Organ, gave Opportunity to them to fix their Lodgment there.

WHEN Persons grew no better for Sweating, but weaker, and the Distemper higher, it was judged fatal.

FOR after Nature had made such an Effort to expel the Venom to no Purpose, all Hopes of Recovery could not but vanish. A great Expence of Spirit, and a general Decay of Strength, must be the Consequence of such a Wast; and a Continuance of Sweat likewise brings on a dangerous Colliquatation, or is a Sign of it; and those hot sharp Sweats, which vesicate the Skin, are also to be suspected: Moreover, it is very hazardous when cold Sweats come after such hot ones. But the most certain Fatality of all, is from such Sweats as have a cadaverous Smell; altho' there was sometimes a very disagreeable scented Sweat, with which they recovered, as with it exhaled the pestilential Venom.

A Loss of Appetite for a great while, proved most commonly but a dangerous Prognostick.

IT appears, by what hath been already said, that a Loathing at Stomach was a certain Sign of Infection; and upon a Continuance of it, it was necessary that there should ensue a Defect of Nourishment and Strength, which made a Person much more liable to the worst Influences of the Distemper, and even to Erosion and Sphacelation of the Stomach.

DEAFNESS joined with Drowsiness, were Signs the Parotides would soon appear.

WHEN Buboes went in again without due Evacuation, and while bad Symptoms continued, Matters were generally doubtful, and for the most Part very dangerous.

I always looked upon my Labours to be defeated, whensoever these Tumours disappeared of a sudden without any manifest Cause; for it was owing to the Retreat of the Venom inwards, where it made terrible Mischief, and was extreamly difficult to be got again to the Surface; yet if Sweats broke out, that the Patient could well bear, it was not uncommon for them to return, and bring again Matters into an hopeful State.

WHENSOEVER these Tumours are discoloured, especially tending to Blackness, or do not suppurate, or are insensible, it may be pronounced the Patient will be worse.

THE more Buboes there are, so that they suppurate, the better.

CARBUNCLES are always more dangerous than Buboes.

BOTH on Account of their sharper Pain, and greater Difficulty to cure.

THE smaller the Carbuncles are in Compass, and their Situation remote from the Viscera, greater Vessels, Tendons, and Nerves, and the fewer they are in Number, by so much it is the better; and, on the contrary, when they spread like a Gangrene, and are near the principal Parts, as the Breast or Belly, and also are numerous, or livid, the Fate of the Patient may be pronounced desperate.

THE pestilential Tokens, especially when they are deep, are the sure and speedy Messengers of Death.

FOR a general Mortification commonly follows these particular ones: although there is sometimes (as before observed) some Time given between one and the other, as for two or three Days.

A Complication of bad Symptoms, together, precipitates the Patient into another World.

NAY, sometimes when there are many Symptoms of Recovery, the obstinate Continuance of one bad is enough to determine the Patient's Fate.

FROM the inconstant Appearance of the Urine, there can be no certain Judgment made.

THE Urine indeed of these Patients is generally not to be distinguished from that of healthful Persons, although sometimes its Stench is not to be endured; this a certain Physician found to his Cost, who taking the Urinal too near, was infected by the Scent, fell ill, and in three Days died.

T H E Pulse, which in all other Diseases is almost a certain Index, in this Sickness could not be at all trusted to.

T H O S E who were comatous in the Beginning or Height of the Disease, seldom escaped.

These Prognosticks I thought my self obliged to take Notice of, by the Method I proposed to my self herein; but that I have omitted many, is to be excused by the Difficulty and Difference of Judgment in these Matters; for such was the delusory Appearance of this Pestilence, that many Patients were lost when they were thought in a safe Recovery; and when we thought the Conquest quite obtained, Death run away with the Victory; whereas others got over it, who were quite given over for lost; much to the Disreputation of our Art.

152

SECTION VII.

Concerning the Cure of the late Pestilence.

A L T H O U G H a pestilential Infection is extreamly dangerous, and doubtful as to its Consequences, very few being spared by it, when in its greatest Height, yet we are by no Means to despair in so great a Difficulty, and give up the whole Race of Mankind to Destruction as soon as it comes, but be rather stimulated to greater Endeavours; and, like faithful Ministers of Nature, study all Helps against such common and grievous Calamities.

B U T before we enter upon that Part which seeks Assistance from Medicine, it may be necessary to exhort the infected, that they have due Regard to the Almighty Power, not only in confessing, and seeking Forgiveness for Sin, but in imploring his Blessing upon those Remedies and Means for Recovery which even the most skilful Physician can prescribe.

153

T H E Infected also ought to be admonished that they make their *Wills*, and settle their worldly Affairs, so as to prevent Contention and Law-Suits, least by the Severity of such a Distemper they should chance to be carried off. But this is to be done before they are affected at all in their Understandings by the Disease.

L A S T L Y , It is likewise to be enjoined the Sick, that they quietly, submissively, and with a chearful Confidence, commit themselves to the Care and Management of their Physicians; And hence appears the Difficulty of that Task to watch over those who are in such imminent Danger; and what variety of Cares lie upon him who undertakes it, and who often falls himself by that Tyrant he is endeavouring to defend others from?

B U T to do Justice to the *Sacred* Art, in its relieving Mankind in such cruel Diseases, this must eternize the Sons of *Esculapius*, that they seem to be born for the Publick Good, by their Usefulness even in a Pestilence, as well as other more common Calamities of Life; but on this Head I shall forbear saying more, knowing how unworthy I am to give due Honour to so much Worth.

154

B U T in the Prosecution hereof, as some heretofore have taken a great deal of Pains to no Purpose in finding an *universal specifick* against the Pestilence, and have imposed many palpable Falsities upon the World under such Pretences; so our modern *Coal-Blowers* have in like Manner cried up their pernicious Secrets, and wickedly imposed them upon the credulous Populace. Certainly these publick Cheats ought themselves to be deemed pestilential, as their Notions and Practice is abhorrent to all sound Reason: For if the Arguments on both Sides the Question be fairly stated, and one will be convinced, that there never as yet hath been discovered in Nature, the full and absolute Essence of a Pestilence, but that it still remains a Mystery to Mankind; wherefore in this Distemper a Person must proceed, as in all others, by a serious Attention to the manifest Symptoms, and a rational Conformity of the Means of Cure thereunto; and while we hold to this only Rule of Procedure, although the Severity of the Distemper may conquer several, yet many also may be saved.

155

I T now comes to us to declare what a Physician has to do in this Calamity; as therefore the Disease admits of no Delays, Help must be immediately procured, and the

Physician ought to fly to the Patient's Succour, least, by any Omission, the Case should be got beyond Recovery, and a Person be lost for Want of timely Assistance.

WHEN the Physician is come, he ought to address the Patient with Chearfulness, and blame those Fears and melancholy Apprehensions which give many over too much into the Power of the Distemper, by cutting off all Hopes of Recovery.

LASTLY, according to the general Directory of our College beforementioned, the most generous and efficacious Medicines must be contrived with the utmost Care and Deliberation.

IN the first Place then, whether Phlebotomy is to be practiced or not is justly to be questioned; and indeed I should pass it by here as fatal, but that I know many unskilful and rash Persons, who not only let Blood largely at one Time, but order it likewise to be repeated until the Patient faints.

BUT if the Authority of the Ancients as well as the Experience of the Moderns hath any Weight, and indeed if our own Practice may be regarded, it is highly to be feared, from many Instances, that Bleeding in a genuine Pestilence is not only to be suspected, but charged as pernicious; for we have many times seen the Blood and Life drawn away together; which makes it astonishing to see the Practisers in such Mischief dare to justifie the fatal Error; what is it that indicates this Evacuation, is it intense Heat; or any Turgescency of the Vessels? Or is it to give Vent to the pestilential Poison to make its escape? Certainly nothing to me seems more absurd; for if the other Symptoms do not remit with the Fever, the Patient will be plunged into the utmost Hazard; for how can the Blood and other Juices be depurated, if the febrile Heat is extinguished? not to say any thing of a Suppression of salutary Breathings hereby, a Perversion of the natural Secretions, and Sinking the Spirits.

THEY also are under as great an Error, who fetch their Reasons for this Practice from the Turgescency of the Vessels; for while inordinate Hurries are excited in the Blood, from disagreeing and heterogeneous Particles striving to extricate themselves from one another, there is made thereby only a seeming Plenitude; what Madness then must it be, in order to remove an imaginary Fulness, to sink the necessary Strength by a rash Effusion of Blood?

AND lastly, the morbifick Poison is not of that kind, as to seek an Escape at the Orifice of a Vein, and run out with the flowing Blood; and which (as before proved) affecting chiefly the Spirits, and residing in other Vessels, makes this Method of Cure in a Pestilence impracticable. I will not however deny but that there may possibly be Circumstances in malignant and pestilential Fevers, which may justifie Phlebotomy, as when it is done for Revulsion sake, in too great a Flux of the *Menses*. But in a genuine Pestilence, it is not to be meddled with. There is but one, as I can remember, who survived it in the late Sickness; but it is needless to say any more upon a Subject so plain, and therefore I shall pass to what is of more Consequence.

AS for what concerns the next Means of Remedy, an *Emetick* may be given in the Infancy of the Disease, where the Stomach is loaded either by over-eating, or by a Crowd of bad Humours, or when there is a Loathing, or a Bitterness in the Mouth; so that any particular Conformation of the Breast and Neck doth not contra-indicate; and amongst these Remedies they are preferable which plentifully excite Vomiting, without working also downwards.

OF this kind are the *Syr. Diasari Vernelij, Syr. Scabios. compos. Oxymel. Scillit.* and chiefly the *Sal Vitrioli*; but the Antimonial Preparations are not so advisable. The Dose of the *Emetick* ought to be large enough to Empty the Stomach soon; and the Posset-drink used in the Operation, in order to rince off its Coats all Filthiness, is to be impregnated with *Carduus, Scordium, Meadow-sweet, Butterbur*, &c. boiled in it. In my own Practice, I have always found good Service from large Draughts of the Posset-drink above-mentioned, sweetned with *simple Oxymel*, without any other previous *Emetick* given.

AFTER Vomiting is over, in order to enable the Stomach the better to keep any Alexipharmick Medicines, its Force may be greatly strengthned by adding Stomachicks to the Alexipharmicks: But if a Reaching to vomit prove Symptomatical, *Emeticks* are by all Means to be avoided; least the Physician (like old Nurses, who are altogether ignorant of the Rules of Practice) should promote that Symptom, which by fruitless Strains waste the Spirits, and sollicit the pestilential Venom into the Stomach from distant Parts; which when fixed there, still irritates into more violent Reachings, that cannot be asswaged by any Remedies.

ALTHOUGH in other Cases a Vomiting may be removed by *Emeticks*, yet in a Pestilence it is dangerous to follow such Practice; because the Malignity, or rather Nitrosaline *Effluvia*, vellicate the Mouth of the Stomach, and so invert its nervous Coats, although empty, as to bring on Convulsions: And some Persons seem to have their Stomachs full, as overloaded 160 with Food, who crave to be freed by Vomiting, which it is by no Means safe to indulge them in, because such a Sensation of Fulness proceeds only from the pestilential Poyson vellicating the Membranes, while the Stomach is it self free from Food, or bad Humours; but what further concerns this Matter, will come to be further considered under the Cure of Symptoms.

MOREOVER, Purges are justly reckoned amongst Medicines of great Efficacy; but whether or no they are to be used in the Case before us, is a Difficulty, and full of Controversy amongst Physicians; and indeed the Varieties in pestilential Diseases, the Differences of Constitutions, the various Complication of Circumstances, the Uncertainty of Seasons, *&c.* do make it impossible to give any general Rules hereupon; wherefore I shall go no further than what my own Practice hath enabled me to judge concerning it.

A Turgescency or Distemperature of Humours do certainly call for an Evacuation this Way; that is, when the Humours are troublesome more by their 161 Quantity than any stimulating Quality; when therefore the Constitution is not able to conquer such a Burthen, neither by Digestion nor Expulsion, Catharticks are certainly necessary to help away the Load, and especially if a Person hath been before eating to Excess.

BUT if this Evacuation be delayed till the Juices have received the pestilential Taint, the Humours are then rather to be depurated, then purged away by Catharticks; and it is certainly better to trust to the Strength of Nature, when Things are gone so far, to do the Work her own Way: And whether or no the Blood is too much fused, or (according to some) coagulated, purging Medicines are certainly to be avoided; for in the first Case they further agitate and fuse the Blood, besides the Hazard of breaking open such Vessels as may not without great Difficulty be again closed; the same Medicines are also hurtful in the Blood's Coagulation, because they evacuate only the serous Parts, and leave the Remainder more viscid and tenacious, whereby Obstructions are rendred more perverse and unconquerable, and the stagnant Matter without a Possibility of Dilution, 162 and Restitution to its pristine State of Fluidity, as also more strongly inclosing the pestilential Poison at the same Time; it is also greatly to be feared, that in so great an Agitation the morbifick Venom may be drawn to the Bowels, and Sphacelation follow thereupon.

THAT Purging may be also practised with Success, the Strength of the Patient is carefully to be consulted, for where the Spirits are low, or deficient, it may not only prove unsafe, but fatal; and where the Bowels are extreamly stimulated by the Cathartick, and the Humours greatly put into Fusion by its rarifying Qualities, they will be apt to pass off in too large a Profusion.

WHAT can a Person likewise expect to do with a Cathartick, in Disorders of the Spirits? It certainly appears to me more likely to purge away all the Humours of the Body, than re-kindle the Spirits that are oppressed, cloudy, and almost extinct, by such Means; and further, as the Subtilty of the pestilential Poison inclines it rather to escape by the superficial Pores, than the larger Emunctories, this Method 163 is contrary to that natural Tendency, calling it back again from the Circumference to the Center; I cannot imagine what they propose, who even repeat in these Cases their purging Medicines, until they bring both intolerable Pains, and Gripings into the Bowels, and Sphacelations, as beforementioned.

BUT if after all Considerations any Person thinks it proper to purge, it ought to be certainly done in the Beginning of the Infection, and with somewhat that operates speedily; and to which Purpose those in Liquid Forms answer best, as for Example:

℞ *Aq. Angelicæ simpl. Tartarizatæ* ℥ ij. *Syr. de spinâ Cervinâ* ℥ j. *Elix. proprietatis Crollii vel Antipestilentialis* ℈ j. *& interdum* ʒ [ss.]dissolve *salis absynthii gr.* viij. *M. S. Fiat haustus horâ commodâ, & typo remittendo dandus.*

A Solution also of *Pil. Ruffi* from ʒ [ss.] to ʒ j. may be made in *Marigold Water*, by those who like that better. They who please likewise may use the following:

℞ *Extract. Pilularum Ruffi* ʒ ij. *resin zalapii* ℈ j. *trochisc. de rhabarb.* ʒ j. *gum. ammoniaci* 164 *in aceto scillit. soluti* ʒ j. *salis Tartari, absynthii* ana gr. viij. *cum tinct. Theriacali q. s. fiat massa, è cujus* ʒ j. *conglobentur pilulæ* vij., *vel* viij. *Dos. in constitutione athleticâ ad* ℈ ij. *prout medico visum fuerit varianda.*

I N a Disease that will admit of no Delay, it is best to evacuate but little, yet that not slowly; so that the morbid Humours may be expelled at the first Seizure, before they have received the pestilential Taint, and before its Virulence hath reached to the whole Mass of Fluids: For it is certain that no Digestion is to be expected in this Case, and therefore can there be no Room for *Alterants* or *Digestives*: But when the Body is very costive, I judge it most convenient and safe to do this with Suppositories.

B U T all Authors and practical Physicians agree in this, to throw out the pestilential Malignity as soon as possible; which is expeditiously and surprizingly done by *Alexipharmicks*; and to these, as soon as the Belly is loosned, Recourse must speedily be had, as to a sacred Refuge: And there is such Plenty of Remedies of this kind, that Nature seems to have had more than 165 an ordinary Indulgence and Forecast, in providing against this destructive Enemy of Mankind; nor hath the medicinal Art been likewise wanting in supplying us with many Preparations of *Simples*, that are powerful against so grievous a Destroyer. But in this great Choice it behoves us to select those which are most efficacious; for this Distemper, which is certainly the most tyrannical of any that besets a humane Body, may be sometimes conquered in its Infancy, which when got to a Head, is not to be managed by the greatest Efforts of humane Skill.

A M O N G S T the Simples of the three Kingdoms, to begin with the Vegetable, *Virginian Snake Root*, when fresh and fragrant, is the most efficacious; insomuch indeed that I have often admired, that such great Vertue should reside in such minute Fibres, having a Tast very pungent, and a quick aromatick Scent, and discovering somewhat wonderful and almost supernatural; so that it deservedly is accounted the most efficacious and generous *Diaphoretick* and *Alexipharmick* for expelling the pestilential Poison. Its Dose, finely powdered, is from gr.iv. or vi. to ℈ ij. in any proper Vehicle, 166 due Regard being had to the Strength and Age of the Patient.

T H E next Place is justly given to the *Contrayerva-Root*, from which also a compound Medicine, which I shall hereafter describe, is admirably contrived: The Dose of this in fine Powder is from ℈ i. to ʒ i. in *Angelica*, or *Scordium* Water, or in Wine, &c.

T H E R E are other Roots likewise which daily Experience hath taught us to be very good for the same Purposes; and with which, as Occasion requires, many valuable Compounds are formed, in order to effect that with a united Force which they could not do singly; in this Class are the Roots of *Angelica, Scorzonera, Butterbur, Masterwort, Tormentil, Zedoary, Garlick, Elicampane, Valerian, Birthwort, Gentian, Bittany*, and many others, which any Person that loves Variety may find in proper Authors.

B U T even Gratitude obliges me not to omit saying somewhat of *Ginger*, which I have prescribed both in the Root powdered, and candied, many Times with great 167 Success, for it is very powerful both to raise a breathing Sweat, and defend the Spirits against the Pestilential Impression.

F R O M these Roots may be made Extracts, either with Spirit of Wine or Vinegar; for it is agreed by all, that the more subtil Particles collected together, and divested of their grosser and unprofitable Parts, become more efficacious in Medicinal Cases.

T H E Leaves of Vegetables most used in Practice, are *Scordium, Rue, Sage, Veronica, Dragon*, the *lesser Centaury, Scabious, Pimpinel, Marygolds* and *Baum*, and from which, on Occasion, are several *Formulæ* contrived.

G O O D Vehicles to wash down and facilitate the taking more efficacious Medicines, are made of the Waters distilled from those Herbs while they are fresh and

40

fragrant (having not yet lost their volatile Salt;) for those which are commonly kept for Ornament in the Shops are insipid, and of little or no Worth.

A *Clyssus* also of the same Herbs is preferable to the Waters, made after 168 this Manner, let a Quantity of Water be drawn from the green and succulent Plant, and the Juice be expressed from another Parcel of the same Herb, and depurated by standing; let then both be evaporated to the Consistence of *Honey*, and from it a Tincture drawn with some more distilled Water and a little Spirit of Wine, which is again by Evaporation to be reduced into an Extract; also from the dryed Plant draw its essential Oil, and from the *Residium* after Distillation the Salt. Of the Extract take ℥ iv. of the *Salt* ℥ [ss.], and of the *Oil* 50 drops, and mix them together, where let them lie to incorporate more intimately with one another. The inspissated Juices likewise of these Ingredients are of good Effect, and in the Winter, Decoctions may conveniently be made of them for the same medical Purposes; and further, that the Remedies in this Case may be yet the more efficacious, they may be joined with *Alkaline-Salts* dissolved in a proper *Menstruum*. For by this Means the Tone of the Stomach will be strengthened, Putrefaction will be prevented, the nitro-saline *Effluvia* will be resisted, or at least precipitated, and a *Diaphoresis* promoted.

169

SOME Berries are also of great Use in Practice; as the Powder of *Ivy-Berries* given to the Quantity of one Dram in two Parts of *Elder Vinegar*, and One Part of *White-Wine*; the Spirit likewise drawn from *Elder-Berries* would do the same in a Dose of ℥ iij. or ℥ iv. the Spirit of *Juniper Berries* given to ℥ i. a Spirit drawn from green *Walnuts*, with *Treacle-Water*, as also from the Seeds of *Carduus*, *Citrons*, &c. had likewise their due Recommendations in powerfully promoting Sweat.

BUT I know nothing amongst the *Simples* that hath so obtained, for Ages together, as the *Oriental Bezoar*, and which still hath so great a Name; yet without having any Inclination to contradict a received Opinion, I have been so confirmed by a Multitude of Trials, that the Truth will speak for it self, which manifestly denies its Virtues to be at all equivalent to its Value: And I have really given it in Powder many times to 40 or 50 Grains, without any manner of Effect; and I dare affirm that the *Bezoar* with which I made these Trials was genuine.

170

THE Powder also of an *Unicorn*'s Horn, so much cried up for an Antidote, never answered any good Expectations, although I had several Dozes of it given me by a Merchant, on purpose to try its Virtues: But that which would cure Pidgeons, Fowls, Cats and Dogs, from Arsenical Poisons, as the worthy Gentleman assured me that did, had yet no Efficacy against the pestilential Virulence: Yet if it was not controverted to this very Day, whether or no there is such an Animal in Being as an *Unicorn*; and it should moreover be granted that the Horn hath these stupendious Virtues; the Price of it would make it purchaseable only by the Rich; whereas in this dreadful Calamity the Populace were chiefly infected; and therefore cheap and common Medicines should be contrived for them by the Physicians; in the Number of which, first occur the *Troches* of *Vipers*, given to the Quantity of ℈ iv. in compound *Scordium Water*, or the volatile *Salt* of *Vipers* given to ℥ [ss.] in the same Vehicle. A very worthy Person sent us from *New-England* some Troches made of the Flesh of a *Rattle-Snake*, from which I found more Success amongst the Sick, than those we commonly have here.

171

THE *Powder of Toads* was likewise prodigiously extolled by every Body; but I found more Success in *Spirits of Hartshorn*, given from ℈ ij. to ℥ i. in *Plague-water*.

A Youth was seized with a great Difficulty of Breathing, and the Arteries hardly beat, and, in short, all Things seem'd to bespeak him in his last Moments; I prescribed him ℥ i. of the forementioned Spirits in ℥iij. of *compound Scordium Water*, but the Symptoms continuing obstinate, I again repeated the same in three Hours Time with Addition of ℈ i. more; and five Blisters were also forthwith applied, after which in about half an Hour, he began to move his Limbs, and recollect himself, as if risen from the Dead: but at last when all Things were hopeful, there appeared a Discolouration upon one of his Legs, where a Blister had been raised, with a Loss of Sense very near to a Sphacelation; upon this the affected Part was deeply scarified and then fomented, which, with a Repetition of the same Draught twice in a Day, by the Blessing of Heaven, again restored every Thing into a hopeful Way. For this Spirit is of such a fiery Nature,172 that it immediately disperses through the whole Body; and on Account of its great Volatility, helps to encounter with, and correct the saline, malignant Quality of the Pestilence: But I need say no more than that it is the most powerful *Diaphoretick* that can be given in any Disease whatsoever.

WHENSOEVER Things are brought to Extremity, some have Recourse to Mineral Preparations, in Order to drive out the Pestilence by mere Force; amongst which the chief are *Mineral Bezoar, Sulphur Auratum,* and *Aurum Vitæ,* &c. the Preparations of which are to be met with in chymical Writers.

I am fearful indeed of being too prolix in the Enumeration of Remedies under this Class; although I am very sensible that some *Simples* prudently chosen may singly encounter a Pestilence with Success, as well as some other Diseases: But because this Evil is usually attended with so many Complications, the Contrivances to oppose it should also, in the Opinion of some, be equally and proportionably complicated; and all Forces drawn up in Battle173 against it with full Front, in Order to be equal to the Encounter. To this Purpose some of the Sons of *Esculapius* have invented manifold Compositions; and some of them so prolix, as if they intended a Sacrifice of an *Hecatomb* to appease the Severity of this tyrannical Destroyer.

IT would be entirely foreign to our Business here, to extract all the Medicines which some Writers abound with for this End; and it is our Business here only to take Notice of those which were made Use of with Success in the late Sickness; and in this Performance both Gratitude and Duty oblige me to begin with such as were ordered by the *College,* amongst which first occurs their *Plague-water.*

℞ Radic. *tormentilla, angelicæ, pæoniæ, zedoariæ, glycirrhizæ, helenii* ana ʒ [ss.] *sol. Salviæ, Chelidoniæ, rutæ, summitat: rorismarini, absynthii, roris solis, artemisiæ, pimpinellæ, dracunculi, scabiosæ, agrimoniæ, melissæ, cardui, betonicæ, centaurii min. fol. & flor. calendulæ* ana M i. *(alii addunt flor. papaveris errat: paralys. ana p.*iij.) *incisa, & contusa infundantur per triduum in lib.* viij. *vin. alb. opt. dein V. cauta distillatio & liquor usui reservetur.* But here it is by174 the Way to be taken Notice, that in the Cure of a Pestilence the medicinal Forms are not to be pompously contrived with a long Catalogue of Ingredients, but carefully adapted in every Respect to the Circumstances and Exigencies of the Infected. It is also to be observed, that this Water is by no Means indifferently to be given to all; or to every one in the same Manner; as for Instance, not at all to Women under their menstrual Purgations, least it should provoke them to flow too immoderately; nor is it to be allowed to Women with Child, for Fear of Miscarriage.

MOREOVER the *College* hath appropriated other Medicines for the same Ends, from which we may extract the following:

℞ *Diascordii, vel Mithridatii* ʒ j. *vel* ʒ [ss.] *fiat dissolutio in lib.*[ss.] *possetalæ alteratæ cum partibus aq. vini albi, & aceti opt. Misce detur hæc potio servefacta, ægro stragulis benè cooperto.* Or,

℞ Radic. *Angelicæ* ʒ ij. *tormentillæ* ʒ j. *infusis, & decoctis in aq. font. q. s. ad tertiæ p. consumptionem, adde succi limonum* ʒ iij. *vel aceti* ʒ j. [ss.] *bibat correptus* ʒ vij, *vel* viij. *hujus apozematis calefacti.* Or,

℞ *Sem. pætasitidis* Э j. *sem. citri gr.* xxvj. *cuchianellæ* Э [ss.] *caphuræ gr.* xij. *misce, fiat pulvis, ex haustu aq. cardui, calendulæ, vel scordii sumendus.* Or,

℞ *Expressionem stercoris vaccini recentis in aceto acerrimo infusi ad cochl.* vij. *vel* viij. Or,

℞ *Theriacæ Androm.* Э ij. *Elect. de ovo vulg.* ʒ [ss.] *factâ dissolutione in haustu possetalæ carduatæ, fiat potio, bibatur calefacta expectando sudoris exsudationem.*

WE shall hereafter come to take Notice of those Medicines which by the *College* were contrived for the Poor, now therefore take those which by daily Experience were found of most Efficacy, and deserve to stand first on that Account.

A Compound Antipestilential Decoction.

℞ *Radic. Scorzonerœ, petasitidis ana* ℥ v. *angelicœ, tormentillœ C.C.C. ana* ℥ j. *fol. Scordii, ulmariœ, melissœ ana* M j. *flor. calendulœ, borrag. ana* M fs. *bacc. juniperi, hederœ ana* ℥ j. *sem. citri* ʒ ij. *coriandri prœp* ʒ. j. fs. *caricas numero* iij. *incisa, & prœp. in duabus p. aqu. font.* 176 *& tertia p. aceti opt. infundantur, & decoquantur, sub finem addendo glycyr. taleolatim sectœ* ℥ j. *in expressionis lib.* iij. *dissolve theriacœ Androm.* ℥ iij. *nitri purissimi* ʒ iij. *& adms. interdum Spir. Vitrioli, vel Sulph. guttas aliquot ad leriusculam aciditatem.* Sometimes also we add hereunto Syrup of the Juice of *Citrons,* or *Baum;* but when Matters are in the utmost Hazard, the Patient's Life is more to be consulted than his Palate; and all *Sugars* we often omit, as they are both a Load upon the Medicin's Operation, and in no wise fit for a Stomach affected with a Contagion. The Dose of this Decoction is from 8 to 10 Spoonfuls every 4 Hours.

An Alexiterial Water.

℞ *Radic. Contrayerva* ℥ j. *scorzonerœ hispan. angelicœ ana* ℥ j. [ss.] *fol. Scordii galegœ ana* M iij. *fl. ros. rubr. calendulœ ana p.* iij. *ras. C. C. eboris ana* ℥ j. *bacc. juniperi, hederœ ana* ℥ ij. *in aceto sambucino per triduum macerat: dictamni cretici, cortic. limonum ana* ℥ j. *succ. melissœ, cardui, angelicœ ana lib.* [ss.] *aceti opt. lib.* ij. *distilla in organis humilioribus post. deb. infusionem.* Or,

℞ *Succ. Scordii, acetosœ ana lib.* j. *galegœ lib.* [ss.] *succ. limonum, aceti opt. ana lib.* j. *theriac.* 177 *Androm.* ℥ iij. *digere & distilla Dos. ad cochl.* vj. *vel* viij.

Or,

℞ *Aquœ Alexiteriœ lib.* ij. *theriac. Androm.* ℥ iij. *Elect. de oro* ℥ j. *digere, filtra, & usui serva, Dos. ad cochl.* vj. *vel* viij. *phiœlam agitando.*

Or,

℞ *Summit absynthij, rutœ ana* M j. *Scordii, dracunculi ana* M iij. *aceti sambuc.* lib. iij. *distilla in vesicâ, tum in liquore dissolve salis fraxini, carduii, vel Scordii Vitriolat.* ʒ iij. *Dos. ad cochl.* iv. *vel* v. *efficaciter elicit sudorem hœc Aqua.*

A Treacle-Water.

℞ *Radic. Asari Virgin.* ℥ [ss.] *contrayerva* ℥ j. *tormentillœ, scorzon. petasitidis ana* ℥ j. *p. sem. cardui, calendulœ, angelicœ, citri ana* ʒ iij. *quibus prœp. affunde spir. vini, aceti opt. ana lib.* [ss.] *dissolve theriac. Ven.* lib. [ss.] *adde croci Ang.* ʒ ij. *misce indantur organis vitreis, & post octiduanam super cineres digestionem, distillœ, in rostro Alembici suspendendo caphurœ* ʒ iij. *Dos. ad cochl.* v. *vel* vj.

A Diaphoretick Oil.

℞ *Salis Absynthii, vel Scordii, sive Rutœ* ℥ ij. *flor. Sulphuris ter, quaterve sublimat.* ℥ j. *ol. Juniperi* lib. j. *invicèm misc., per biduum calore mediocri benè occlusa relinque, dein per Retortam distilla, etiam alterâ vice distilla, digerendo per biduum, addendo salis absynthij* ℥ j. *Dos. ad cochl. unum, vel duo, ex aq. angelicœ, vel scordii, saccharatâ, ad olei* v. *a. e. Commixtionem.*

An Alexipharmick Vinegar.

℞ *Radic. Scorzon. Hispan. Chelidoniœ mai. ana* ℥ ij. *contrayerva* ℥ i. *angelicœ, tormentillœ ana* ℥ i. *p. fol. scordii, melissœ, scabiosœ ana* M ij. *summit. Rutœ p.* ij. *dictamni cret.* M [ss.] *flor. sambuci, calendulœ ana p.* iij. *gr. Junip.* ℥ ij. *ras. C. C. eboris ana* ℥ j. *sem. rutœ, cardui, citri ana* ʒ ij. *portulacœ* ʒ v. *cinam. opt.* ℥ [ss.] *caryophyll.* ʒ iij. *Theriac. Androm.* lib. [ss.] *quibus s. a. prœp. affunde Aceti ex vin. albo acerrimi lib.* v. *vitro opt. obaurato digere per triduum, bis, terve de die conquassando, tum cautè distilla, suspensis camphorœ, & croci ana* ʒ ij. *in rostro Alemb. Dos. ad cochl.* v. *vel* vj.

B U T sufficiently of these; from whence it is easie for any one to gather, why liquid Medicines, and especially when warmed, are preferrable to others in the Form of *Boles* or *Electuaries;* that is, because of their more expeditious and more effectual Operations.

B U T because many of the Infected have a Loathing at Stomach, and an Inclination to vomit, in the same Manner as an Overload of Eating and Drinking occasions, Medicines in solid Forms suit best with such, as they are not so easily thrown up, and adhere better to the Sides of the Stomach: Of this Kind we have the following Composition, which at taking may be made into Boles of ʒ ij. each adding thereunto *Salt of Carduus*, or *Wormwood* ϶ j. or more or less according to the Exigency of Symptoms.

℞ *Elect. de ovo mineralis* ʒ j. *theriac. Androm.* ʒ |ss.| *pulv: serpentariæ virgin.* ʒ v. *cuchianellæ* ʒ iij. *croci pulveriz.* ʒ |ss.| *cum Syr. è succo melissophyll. vel citri, coagmentetur massa.*

The famous Sir **Theodore Mayerne**'s *Electuarium de Ovo.*

℞ *Ovum vulgariter ut in Pharmacopœia* Londinensi *præp. de quo sume, & sem. sinapios, vel eruca ana* ʒ j. *Antidoti Saxonicæ* ʒ |ss.| *lapidis prunellæ* ʒ v. *Antimonii diaphoret. fixissimi, & croci metallorum simul ustorum* ʒ iij. *pulv. scordii, rutæ, zedoariæ ana* ʒ ij. |ss.| *Theriacæ ven. veteris* ʒ iv. *Philonii Turneri* ϶ vij. *gr. ij. misce & cum spir. Theriac.* ʒ iij. *& mellis de spumati q. s.* Fiat *Elect. molle, Dos. ad* ϶ iv. *vel* ʒ ij. *corroborand. adjiciendo corda, & jecinora* vj. *viperarum v. a. e. præp.* But it is to be observed in this likewise, as in other Antidotes, that a long Fermentation of the Ingredients together in a Mass is very necessary, because by that Means they more intimately mix with one another.

BUT if the Body be too open, the *Lapis Contrayerva* is very suitable, and 'tis thus made:

℞ *Pulv. radic. contrayerva res.* ʒ j. *serpentariæ virgin.* ʒ ij. |ss.| *extract. radic. Angelicæ, tormentillæ ana* ʒ ij. *pulv. C. C. philosophicè calcin. chelarum Cancrorum præp. pulv. Corall. rubr. ana* ʒ j. |ss.| *Antimonii Diaphoret. vel potius Diaphor. Jovis* ʒ iij. *cuchianellæ* ʒ |ss.| *croci* ϶ j. *(aliqui addurat lapid. bezoar. orien.* ϶ ij.) *ambræ grys.* ϶ |ss.| *cum gelatinâ spoliorum serpentum. vel C. C. fingantur globuli s. a. exiccandi, Dos. ad* ϶ ij. *vel* ʒ j. *è vehiculo idoneo.* &c.

FOR the same Purpose also is the celebrated *Orvietan* thus compounded, and given ʒ ij. at a Dose.

℞ *Cardui bened. totius eupatorii maj. & min. ana* ʒ |ss.| *scordii, aristolochiæ utriusque ana* ʒ v. *viperinæ, h. e. echii, gentianæ, bacc. Junip. bistortæ ana* ʒ j. *bacc. lauri, tormentillæ, dictamni albi ana* ʒ |ss.| *carlinæ, angelicæ ana* ʒ j. |ss.| *rhabarb. imperatoriæ, scorzon. hispan. valerianæ ana* ʒ |ss.| *morsus diaboli, calami aromat. ana* ʒ iv. *Theriac. Androm. opt.* ʒ iij. *corda, & jecinora* 12 *viperarum, terantur terenda subtilissimè, & cum s. q. mellis despumati fiat Elect. per tres menses fermentand.*

IT is to be observed, that these and the like Medicines, whether *Galenical* or *Spagyrical*, which cannot be prepared as soon as *Asparagus* can be boiled, ought to be always in Readiness.

THE general Remedies being thus provided, the exact Way of Living and Diet comes to be considered: And first of all whensoever the Patient is taken, he must immediately be put to Bed; wherein we have found it much more serviceable to be covered with Blankets, than Linen Sheets, because the Woollen much better encourages Sweating, and also absorps it, and keeps the Body cleaner all the while; for Linen being not suited to drink up the Sweat, the Pores of the Body, at such Times as open as possible, will be choaked up and obstructed by the Moisture hanging upon the Skin, and giving also a Chilliness to the Flesh: To all therefore who sweat thus, Change of Cloaths is to be denied, for the Patient takes Harm by clean Coverings, not so much from any prejudicial Quality of the Soap abounding in them, (according to the Opinion of *Diemebrooeck*) as from a Dampness which is inseparable from them, and the Approach of Air which is unavoidable in the Shifting; both which will check the Sweating.

UNLESS the Patient hath Occasion for a Vomit, or Purge, or a Clyster, immediately upon his going to Bed, *Alexipharmicks* ought to be given, and if thrown up by Vomiting, repeated until the Stomach if strengthned, and can retain them; and I have always observed, that such Nauseousness goes off as soon as Sweat breaks out.

SOME indeed of a very dry Temperament, or from a Consumption of their Humidities by the febrile Heat, do not easily get into a Sweat; such therefore I ordered liberally to drink of a medicated Posset-Drink; in order by this Means both to render the viscid Humours more fluid, and contemper and asswage the feverish Heat.

THE Milk with which this Posset-Drink was made, was turned with two Parts of Ale, and one Part of Vinegar, in which had been boiled the Roots of *Scorzonera* and *Butterbur*; the Leaves of *Baum*, *Scabius*, and *Wood-sorrel*; the Flowers of *Borage* and *Marygolds*; the Raspings of *Ivory* and *Hartshorn*, and *Carduus* and *Coriander* Seeds.

THESE Sweats we used to keep up for two or three Hours at a Time, as the Strength would bear them; and until the 184 morbifick Venom was rarified and subtilized, so as to be exhaled quite away along with the viscid Humours: Sleep also was industriously kept off, although sometimes, through meer Weariness, the Patient would drop into a Doze.

AS much Care, besides that of Sweating them, was taken to support the Strength and Spirits of the Infected, by such Aliments as the Stomach was able to receive; for which End I ordered them Bread soaked in Wine, poached Eggs with *Juice of Citrons*, *Pomegranates*, or *Elder Vinegar*, as also cordial Waters, Broths, Gellies, and sometimes also generous Wines.

THE Broths then used were made by boiling in Chicken-Broth the Roots of *Scorzonera*; the Leaves of *Pimpinel*, *Meadow-sweet*, *Wood-Sorrel*, *Borage*, Raspings of *Hartshorn*, and *Dactyls*, with a Piece of White Bread, and a little *Saffron* tied in a Nodule; and the Fat was not taken off unless in a Loosness or Loathing at Stomach: Of the Usefulness of Gold boiled in these Things I have nothing to say: Of this Broth was also sometimes Emulsions made with the *Seeds of Citrons*, *Plantain*, blanched *Almonds*, and *Pearl-Sugar*.

185

Mayerne's *celebrated Cordial-water.*

℞ Radic. carlinæ ʒ vj. zedoariæ, scorzoneræ, imperatoriæ, gentianæ, vincetox. valerianæ, tormentillæ, bistortæ, petasitid. dictamni, bardanæ, pimpinella totius ana ʒ iv. fol. cardui, oxytriphyll. scordii, ana M v. ulmariæ, scabiosæ, morsus diaboli, melissæ, pentaphyll. menthæ, rutæ, buglossæ, flor. calendulæ, hyperici ana M iv. limones, & Aurant. cum corticibus ana numero xx. flor. salviæ, rorism. ana M ij. corda vervecina numero vj. corda viper. numero xx. vini generosi Hispan. lib. xx. infusione deb. peractâ, fiat Distillatio cauta in B. M. hujus Aq. Dos. ad cochl. iv. vel v. dulcor. (si ita visum) cum sacchari perl. q. s.

BUT the Patients were kept from Aliments of this Kind until some Relief was found by *Alexipharmicks*; and then only so much was allowed of as their Strength would admit of, for that was to be helped, and not loaded; but as they grew better, more was allowed: Yet an Hour or two after such Refreshment, notwithstanding the Distemper seemed to be extinguished, *Alexipharmicks* were repeated, until all Suspicion of its Remainder was removed; because 186 sometimes it would on a sudden recruit after it had seemed to be quite gone.

THE Infected were kept close in their Beds the whole Time of the Disease; and those who would not be thus governed, bitterly repented of their Obstinacy; for upon Checking a *Diaphoresis*, and Confining the pestilential Venom, most grievous Pains and Disorders ensued: And they who were delirious, were tied in their Beds, to prevent their doing either Injury to themselves, or those who attended upon them.

IF a Drowsiness came on at the first Attack of the Distemper, or in the Beginning to Sweat, the Patient was forcibly kept awake; although, when some Appearance came of Recovery, a little Sleep was indulged to recruit the Spirits, but not beyond four Hours together; for if they slept longer, they were waked to take their Medicines.

IF the Belly was costive, and the Distemper on its Declension, Clysters were used with Benefit; made of a Decoction with the Roots of *Scorzonera*, *Tormentil*, and *Marsh-Mallows*; the Leaves of *Scordium*, *Meadow-sweet*, 187 and *Violets*; Flowers of *Chamomil* and *Elder*; sweet *Fennil-Seeds*, and *Anniseeds*; and in it was dissolved the Yolk of an *Egg*, brown *Sugar*, and ʒ iij. of *Diascordium* or *London Treacle*; and when more Haste was required for Evacuation, ʒ j. or ʒ j. [ss.] was added of the Infusion of *Crocus Metallorum*. After the Clyster came away, the Patient was allowed a Draught of generous Wine, or of some Cordial Julap, or Broth, &c.

AND whereas a Languor upon the Spirits very much contributed (as before observed) both to the Propagation and Violence of the Contagion; to remove such an Inconvenience, grateful Scents were made use of, such as are known to comfort the Brain;

45

sometimes *Vinegar of Roses* was sprinkled upon live Coals, and at others, were burnt such things as *Styrax*, *Labdanum*, &c. of which more hereafter, and all things avoided which might give any Offence to the Nose by its Smell.

HITHERTO we have treated of Antidotes, and the Regimen of our Patents; next we come to external Helps, amongst which *Blisters* demand the first mention; and whose frequent and successful Application[188] removed all Controversie about their Usefulness.

BLISTER-*Plasters* were applied to several Parts; as the Nape of the Neck, within-side the Arms, the Thighs, and Legs; and by these the Vessels were warmed, the Juices rendered more fluid, a *Stimulus* given to the Sluggishness of Nature, and Passage made sufficiently large, for the Evacuation not only of superfluous Serosities and noxious Humours, but also for the pestilential Poison, which by this Artifice seemed to be turned out this Way; not to say any Thing of the Revulsion made hereby of Venom from the nobler Parts.

FOR this Purpose, I once ordered a *Blister-Plaster* to be applied within-side the Thigh, a little below a Buboe in the Groin, but by the Carelesness of the Nurse, it was laid upon the Buboe it self; which happening to prove fortunate, after obtained in Practice, in Expectation thereby to prevent the morbifick Humour from going back again, and to forward its Suppuration; but altho' this was of Advantage in some Cases, it was yet much suspected by the more cautious Physicians and Surgeons, as for the most Part it[189] brought too great an Inflammation all round it, and promoted a Strangury, which, by Excess of Uneasiness, greatly wasted the Spirits, and sunk the Patient's Strength.

THAT these Applications may certainly answer their End, the most sharp ought to be used: The following Composition never failed me in all my Practice; but before its Application, the Part was always rubbed with Vinegar.

R *Picis navalis* ℥ v. *galbani colat.* ℥ j. *ceræ* ℥ j. |ss.| *quibus simul liquatis, & ab igne semotis, adde pulv. cantharidum præp.* ʒ vij. *vel* ℥ j. *fermenti veteris, sem. ameos ana* ʒ iij. *euphorbii* ʒ j. *cum aceti scillit. q. s. incorporentur, assiduè agitando, quoùsque cogantur in Emplastri massam.*

THE Parts thus vesicated were never suffered to heal, till the Malignity of the Disease was spent; and to prevent their suddain drying up, they were continually stimulated by *Melilot* Plasters sprinkled over with some Powder of *Cantharides*; which kept up a constant Drein of noxious Humours; but to asswage the great Heat and Inflammations, sometimes occasioned hereby, *Cole-wort* Leaves were applied to them.

[190]

YET although *Epispasticks* did so much Service to the Infected, and sufficiently made amends for the Trouble and Pain they gave; yet they were not indifferently suitable to all Persons; As for Instance, where there was an Heat of Urin, or a continual Inclination to piss, where the *Sphincter* of the Bladder was inflamed, or ulcerated, in an Hemorrhage, or to Women with Child, or having the *Menses*; and lastly, where there was a great *Languor* upon the Spirits; it is also diligently to be considered when *Epispasticks* are applied to Buboes or Carbuncles near upon Suppuration, that they do not fuse the Humours too much, to admit them going into a laudible *Pus*, and give such a *Stimulus* to the Parts, as may sink the Spirits, and frustrate other Endeavours of Nature to help her self.

BESIDES *Epispasticks*, it is not lost Labour to apply proper Things to the Feet; I commonly used a Plaster made of the compound *Bettany* Plaster, adding to it some *Euphorbium*, *Saffron*, and *London Treacle*; And I found this to do more Good than *Cataplasms*, which some, however, liked better to use, and were made of *Bryony* Root steeped in[191] Vinegar, the Flesh of *pickled Herrings*, *black Soap*, *Rue*, *Scordium*, and *Arum*, with a sufficient Quantity of Vinegar: Sometimes also Pidgeons were applied to the Feet.

BUT these, and other Medicines of the same Rank, were not applied in any Expectation to draw away by them the pestilential *Miasmata* as by Attraction; but because the Multitude of Pores, and their Largeness in the Soles of the Feet, gave such Things an Opportunity of sending in that warmth, as would keep the Animal Humours more fluxile, and cherish the natural Heat that was almost extinct; and from thence the whole Body would be refreshed by their Influence: Applications were likewise made to the Wrist with the same View.

46

A N D thus having gone through the curative Part of a Pestilence in general, we now come to the Management of particular Symptoms; and first of all of the Buboes.

I T highly concerns all who are concerned for the Sick in these Cases, both Physicians and Surgeons, to attend with Diligence to the Nature of these Tumours, and have their several Differences ready in their Minds, that at their first Sight they may know their Condition, and use Means of treating them accordingly. And first of all it is to be enquired, whether they are moveable or fixt? whether soft or hard? whether depressed or prominent? whether small or great? whether contracted or broad? whether with, or without Pain? and lastly, whether inflamed or not?

W H E N S O E V E R a Buboe is uncertain and dodges, sometimes appearing and then again going back, all Means is to be used to fix it; and this is very successfully done by cupping upon the Glands, which will fix a permanent Tumour upon them.

T O Buboes just in their first Formation, we have indeed applied *Discutients*, and very powerful ones too, in Order to dissipate them; and although they have several Times endeavoured to settle, yet we have not despaired to conquer the Enemy this Way: But we always found it for certain, that they who went through such Fluxes and Refluxes of the pestilential Venom, never recovered in such a perfect Manner, as they whose Buboes immediately fixed, and after Suppuration threw out a great deal of Matter.

I f the Tumour is hard and painful from too great a Tension upon the glandulous Parts, not giving Room enough to receive the protruding Humours, the Part affected may be anointed with *Oil of Lilies, Roses,Elder*, &c. if no Inflammation forbids such a Method; in which Circumstance all Oils and Ointments are to be suspected, as they obstruct the Pores, and are no Ways suitable to the Nature of the nitro-saline pestilential Venom. When an Inflammation therefore is upon any Part, which is easie to be known by its Heat and Colour, it is better to make Use of the *Mucelages of Linseed* and *Fenugreek*, with *Elder Vinegar*, and *London Treacle*; or a *Cataplasm of Wheat-Flower,Fenugreek* and *Linseed, Elder Flowers*, white *Bread Crumbs*, the *Yolk of Eggs*, and *Powder of Saffron*.

T H E London Physicians at this Time spared no Trouble nor Application, to manage the Buboes rightly; some of the Cataplasms therefore by them daily used I shall here insert.

R *Cæpam majusculam, quam v. a. e. excavatam imple summit. rutæ deb. exiccat. & pulveriz.* ℥ ij. *indantur etiam theriac.* Lond. ℈ iv. *foramen operculo suo obturetur, cæpa deinde chartâ bibulâ involuta sub cineribus assetur, cui adde ficum methodo eâdem assatam, cum ol. lini, liliorum alb. ana q. s. simul macerentur, & conficiatur* cataplasma, *applicandum calidè, bis de die immutandum.* This is also good against the Bites of venomous Creatures.

Or,

R *Fol. rutæ, scordii contus. ana* M [ss.] *medullæ carnis ficuum* ℥ ij.*flor. meliloti p.* [ss.] *salis marini pulveriz.* ℥ ii. *fermenti veteris* ℥ [ss.]*cum s. q. aceti, paretur Cataplasma.*

Or,

R *Rad. liliorum, althææ, cum aceto macerat: ana lib.* [ss.] *sem. lini, fænugræci ana* ℥ [ss.] *carnis ficuum* ℥ iij. *confectionis sinapi, cum theriac. ana* ℥ [ss.] *axungiæ suillæ q. s. F. cataplasma.* Or, according to*Mayerne*, from whom I learned the Rudiments of Practice.

R *Succ. apii* ℥ ij. *melissæ* ℥ j. *pimpinellæ* ℥ j. [ss.] *cæpas majores Numero duas, ad intenerationem, sive putrilaginem sub cineribus cautè assatas, alliorum bulbos Numero* vj. *clavos juglandium maj. retust. Numero* iv. *tritis alii bulbis, & clavis, affunde succos, tum adde Cæpas, in mortario marmoreo cum aceti scillit. q. s. agitentur, & cogantur in Cataplasmatis consistentiam.*

B U T the Hardness, pricking Pain, and intense Heat of the Tumour continuing, Medicines were used to dissolve such Hardness, and asswage the Pain and Heat: As,

R *Rad. liliorum alb.* ℥ ij. *porrorum, medullæ carnis ficuum ana* ℥ j.*sem. lini* ℥ [ss.] *flor. Sambuci, meliloti ana p.* [ss.] *micarum panis alb.*lib. [ss.] *coq. in s. q. lactis, addendo sub finem ol. ros. liliorum alb. vel sambuc ana q. s. ut F.* Cataplasma.

Or,

R *Fol. Scabiosæ, acetosæ ana* M ij. *chartâ bibulâ involut. & cineribus scintillantibus subditorum, quibus adde fermenti veteris* ℥ ij.*salis tantillum, agitentur probè in mortario cum s. q. axungiæ suillæ, ad usum præmemoratum.* But that I may not be too tedious in reciting particular Forms of this Kind, any necessary Variations are left to the Discretion of every Physician in his own Practice.

WE do not wait for the Suppuration of a Buboe until it breaks of it self, when the Pain and other Symptoms continue very severe without Remission; besides, there would in doing so be Danger of wasting the Spirits too much, and letting the morbifick Matter retreat, besides the Smalness of the Orifice, which when they open themselves, is seldom large enough to give due Vent; we therefore open them by Incision, or to prevent Mortification, by a potential Cautery; and for the same Purpose it hath also been many Times found reasonable to mix the milder Causticks with Digestives.

YET although common Experience attests to the Advantage of Cataplasms, as they wonderfully cherish the languid and almost extinguished natural Heat, supple the neighbouring Parts, relax the Skin, and contemper and asswage sharp Humours; yet, I say, because their frequent Repetition is sometimes on many Accounts inconvenient and disagreeable, I used to substitute the following *Cerate* in their Room.

℞ *Emp. Oxycrocci* ℥ iij. *galbani colat gum. curannæ ana* ℥ j. *picis navalis* ℥ ij. *è liquatis simul. cum ol. chamæmeli, & liliorum, v. a. e. F. massa pro empl.* And I am bold enough to affirm, that with this I have prevented the Want of a Surgeon in more than a thousand Instances: But when a Buboe is artificially opened, it is the most proper to do it in some depending Part of the Tumour; taking Care not to wound the larger Vessels and Muscles.

BUT whether a Buboe breaks of it self, or is opened by Incision, it is to be washed and cleansed with a *Lixivium* of *Ashes, Scordium, Betony, Bugloss, Sanicle,* &c. in which also is dissolved some *London Treacle:* And the following Mixture I have found very good for this Purpose, consisting of *Birthwort Root, Myrrh, Aloes,* and *Saffron,* infused in *Spirit of Wine,* and to the strained Tincture, adding a little *Oil of Turpentine.* Furthermore, to promote Digestion, and prevent Putrefaction, the following may be applied:

℞ *Mellis ros.* ℥ i. *terebinth. cum vitello ovi solut.* ℥ [ss.] *theriac. Lond.* ʒ iij. *farinæ tritici* ℥ ij. [ss.] *cum ol. hyperici & sambuc. ana q. s. coq. in Cataplasmatis consistentiam.*

Or,

℞ *Ung. basilic. p. duas, linimenti Arcæi p. Tertiam, ol. terebinth.* ʒ[ss.] *M. S.* But here it is to be observed, that Detergents are by no Means to be used, unless the Ulcer is foul; as also that to appease the Enormity of Pain and Inflammation, by Opiates and Repellers, is a most pernicious Practice, because it drives back the Venom upon the nobler Parts; and also by their frequent Continuation, is a Sphacelation endangered upon the Extremities.

THESE Ulcers are likewise by no Means to be healed up until they are well cleansed, and all the pestilential Symptoms quite disappear. But here I cannot but remark, that these Ulcers do heal much easier than any other when the Venom is fully conquered: And in the Cure, it chiefly concerns the Surgeon to prevent the Lips growing callous, because sometimes that Error is not easily again remedied; when the Ulcer is well cleansed, the ordinary *Sarcoticks* used in the common Method will soon fill up the lost Substance: To prevent Repetition, the *Parotides* are to be treated after the same Manner as Buboes.

AFTER this transient View, our Method now brings us to the Cure of Carbuncles; since therefore these Eruptions have their Rise from a pestilential *Lixivium,* thrown upon several Parts of the Body, and there burning them into an *Eschar,* the Business of a Surgeon herein is directed to three main Intentions.

1. THAT the Carbuncle does not spread too far, like a Gangrene, knowing no Bounds.

2. TO bring it as soon as possible to a Separation; and,

3. TO cure it as carefully as it can be done.

FOR the first Intention, such Remedies are suited which give a Restriction to the Part, so that the venomous Particles cannot spread; and such also as asswage the distempered Heat, and cherish and preserve that which is natural.

48

B U T the Cure of a Carbuncle is varied by its Nature, Progress, and Situation; and is accordingly to be treated sometimes with more, and at others with less Severity. In this Case Benefit is sometimes received from a Cataplasm with roasted *Garlick*, *Soot*, *London Treacle*, and *Oil of Turpentine*; Or,

℞ *Fermenti*   *veteris* ℥ [ss.] *allii*   *assati* ℥ ij. *stercoris*   *columbini* ℥ j.*confec. Sinapi* ℥ v. *euphorbii* ℥ ij. *cum s. q. saponis nigri F. Cataplasma*. But it is to be observed, that in the Application of these Cataplasms, which are very sharp, the utmost Caution must be used, that a Pain is not aggravated thereby beyond the Patient's Power to bear; that the Humours be not colliquated, and thrown upon weaker Parts; and that an immoveable *Eschar* be not made thereby.

W H E N the *Eschar* does not fall off, nor any Signs of Separation appear, Unguents and Oils are not to be blamed; but if the Carbuncle spreads further, it will be necessary to have Recourse to more effectual Means; in which Case neither the Tenderness of Sex or Age is to be regarded. Sometimes the pestilential Venom is to be [201] drawn out by Cupping, or Scarrification, or *Epispasticks*. Sometimes also for the same Purpose is applied the bare Rump of a Fowl, repeated until these Creatures appear not to be hurt by it; for this natural Warmth sooths the vital Heat of the Part it is applied to, and entices away the morbifick Venom through the Pores; Pidgeons used alive, and warm Sheeps Lights, have likewise been observed thus to asswage the Acrimony of this pestilential Virulence.

T H E Eschar is sometimes got off by burning, and sometimes by Incision; I never indeed found any thing more effectual than the actual *Cautery*; and in this Practice of ours we differ not from the celebrated *Concoregius*, who tells us, *pag.* 39. that in his Time they were wont to burn the Carbuncle with a red hot Iron. There are very convenient Instruments amongst the Surgeons for this Operation, which they call the *Button*, being so shaped; but they are of little Service, except the Burning extends to the Compass of the Eruption; and the Iron is by no means to be taken away, until the Patient is sensible of it; but to get off the *Eschar*, the middle Part must be burnt deepest.

[202]

A M O N G S T many other Advantages, I shall mention but a few that are received from the actual *Cautery* in these Cases; for from hence the Parts affected are rendred more firm and strong; hence the Vessels are more astringed; hence the subtil *Miasmata* are rarified and evaporated; hence the Poison is corrected and dried up; and lastly, hence the languishing Heat is quickned; and, not to use many Words, the pestilential Venom seems to be destroyed by Burning, no otherwise than the Bites of poisonous Creatures are cured after the same Manner.

A S for what is done by the Knife, the Infected are certainly as much benefitted by it, as by the actual *Cautery*; especially if the Incision be made deep, and goes to the Root at the Centre; for by this may be made a very expeditious Elevation and Separation of the *Eschar*; and this Means is more particularly to be used where a Gangreen is threatned; but in doing it, great Care must be taken, as before hinted, that there is not made any Effusion of Blood by cutting the larger Vessels, especially the Arteries.

[203]

B U T when this Separation is once finished, whether it be by a Knife, or by Burning, or of its own Accord; the next thing is to peal it off; and this is frequently assisted by moistening it with new Butter, Oil of *Elder*, or Oil of *Lilies*. The *Eschar* is likewise to be loosened gradually, and not too hastily; that is, a kind of Maturation is to be waited for. After the Carbuncle is fallen off, Care must be taken to cleanse away the *Sordes* upon it, and promote Digestion by the Use of suitable Applications; and every thing else carefully managed, as before directed in the Cure of Buboes.

L A S T L Y, Incarning is gradually to be effected, and the Ulcer slowly healed over; for by being too hastily closed, it is not uncommon to find some pestilential *Miasmata* lurking behind, which afterwards prove mischievous, and often fatal, as may easily be gathered from a preceding History, and many others not here mentioned.

B U T because sometimes the Parts where Carbuncles arise, cannot be cleansed conveniently from the morbid Humours, whence the Cure proves slow, or cannot be effected204 at all, the circumjacent Parts at first should be guarded by Defensatives, which would astringe the Laxity upon those Parts, keep the Passages clear, and give Room for the due Motions of the Juices and Spirits, while at the same time they prevent the Exhalation of the natural Heat; But if notwithstanding the utmost Care, Sphacelation comes on, immediate Recourse is to be had to Embrocation, with the following.

℞ *Cinerum absynthii, scordii, cardui, centaurii min. ana* ʒ iij. *è quibus paretur lixivium, indendo flor. chamemeli, sambuci, meliloti ana*M j. *liquoris limpidi* lib. ij. *adde spir. vini opt.* lib. [ss.] *dissolve theriac.* Lond. ʒ ij. M. S. *pro fotu p. affectae bis de die, quàm caladissimè, exin Cataplasma conficiatur è theriac.* Lond. *cum Elix. proprietatis.*

LASTLY, To put an End to this Section, wherein to prevent prolixity, I have studiously avoided all Points of Controversy; I cannot altogether omit the Mention of those skilful and faithful Surgeons, with due Honour, whose Task in this raging Calamity was very hard and dangerous, how they had the Care of all pestilential Tumours and Ulcers, &c. But although some of these fell themselves in205 the Discharge of their Duty to others, yet the Survivors went on chearfully in their Business; and they who lived through the whole, owed a great deal to a Constancy of Mind, as well as to the conservatory Power of Providence.

SECTION VIII.

Of Preservation from a Pestilence.

IT is manifestly much more adviseable to keep off the Invasion of a Pestilence, than to stand its violent and fatal Shocks; and Self-Preservation, as well as the Example of all other wise People, admonishes us to use all possible Endeavours to keep it from us, and guard our selves against it while at a Distance. This Part therefore concerning our Preservation from a Pestilence, regards both the Duty of the Magistrate, and the Care of every Individual; that is to say, it is the Magistrate's Duty, that when the Nature and peculiar Qualities of this Disease are known, and reported by Physicians, such Laws should be provided, as might best conduce to prevent its Spreading, if not to its utter Extirpation.

206

FIRST of all therefore, they ought to be deemed as a kind of Traitors, who frighten the credulous Populace with the Apprehensions of an approaching Plague, by idle and groundless Reports and Predictions; for the Propagation of the late Sickness was too notoriously assisted by this Means, to want any Arguments to prove it.

THE timely Separation also of the infected from the well, is absolutely necessary to be done; because the most sure Way of spreading it, is letting the sick and well converse together. Publick Funerals ought to be forbid, as also all kinds of Meetings, and frequent Intercourses of several Persons together: An Injunction also of Quarentine from infected Places, according to the Custom of Trading Nations, is by any Means not to be omitted, and carefully to be executed.

ALTHOUGH it is looked upon as almost impossible by the most artful Contrivances, and the most prudent Councils, to avoid the Influence of a common Cause; yet the Call of Nature, and the Laws of Self-preservation, demand our utmost Diligence207 and Labour, both in publick and private, to prevent the Encroachment of such a subtile and cruel Destroyer. And it was certainly to this purpose a wise Contrivance of the Magistrates, to constitute two in every Parish daily to visit every Family, and be satisfied whether every one belonging thereunto was well, and free from any Infection.

BUT both the Ancients and Moderns have taken the utmost Pains in contriving to purge the Air, on a Supposition that, in a pestilential Contagion, that is *substantially* infected: But as the Air, as before demonstrated, is only the Lodgment or Vehicle to the pestilential *Miasmata*, which are every Way agitated in it, it does not seem so much to want Depuration on its own Account, as that poisonous Mixture which is joined with it. Indeed the pestilential Particles residing in the Porosities of the Air, may often, without any Change of Figure, for Want of due Agitation, remain and stagnate in it a long Time, so as to be drawn in by the Lungs in Inspiration, and hence from the intimate Mixture and Confusion as it were of both, a Suspicion may be entertained of the Taint coming from a208 Corruption of Air; but of this we have said enough already; and as howsoever this Matter is, a Purgation of the Air is by common Consent called for on all Sides in these Cases, we shall consider this Matter, chiefly in these two Respects.

FIRST, That the pestilential *Seminium* be dislodged; and to this Purpose contribute brisk Winds, especially from the *North*, and the frequent Explosions of great Guns, in the Morning and Evening chiefly; because such Concussions agitate the poisonous *Miasmata*, and not only help to dissipate them; but to change and alter them in those particular Configurations whereby they become so noxious; and it hath been attested by Experience, that an intimate Combination of *Nitre* and *Sulphur* greatly alters the saline Qualities of the pestilential Taint.

SECONDLY, The utmost Diligence is to be used to prevent the pestilential Particles from taking Effect; which is succesfully done by proper Fumigations. *Hippocrates*, the Oracle in Physick, hath left it to Posterity, to kindle Fires in the publick Streets; and these sometimes I conceive[209] may do good; but not as some will have it, by absorbing the pestiferous Humidities, but by diffusing on all Sides a great deal of *Nitre*, which gives a considerable Change to the venomous *Miasmata*; I judge it best therefore that such Fires should be made of resinous Woods, which throw out a clear and unctious Smell, such as *Juniper*, *Fir*, *Oak*, *Ash*, *Elm*, *Chesnut*, &c. but by no Means Coals, which exhale an impure, fetid, and suffocating Sulphur.

BY the Care of the Magistrate also the Streets, Sinks, and Canals, should daily be cleared of all Filth; because Stench and Nastiness are justly reckoned the Entertainers of Infection, and we find the Air to be corrupted frequently from noisome Smells; so that the pestilential Venom cannot but receive additional Strength from such Means.

BUT to be yet more particular about these Fumigations, both to mend the Air, and refresh the Houses that have been infected, they must be composed of such Things as raise and comfort the Spirits that were languishing, with their grateful Flavours; for refreshing Smells are a kind[210] of natural *Pabulum* to the animal Spirits; or they should be of such Substances as by their gummy Viscidity entangle and cover the venomous *Spicula*, so that they cannot act; or, lastly, of such Things as breath out such nitrous Steams, which will either preserve our Bodies from receiving Impurities, or change the Nature of the infectious Particles.

I do not indeed deny, but some ungrateful Smells may be sometimes more convenient than sweet ones, as they fix those Spirits which would otherwise exhale; and a copious Efflux of saline Particles will often keep them from Infection and Injury. But to reduce these into Classes.

The *Simples* of the first Class are *Musk*, *Civet*, *Amomum*, *Lavender*, *Rosemary*, *Roses*, *Angelica*, *Marjoram*, *Cloves*, *Rhodium Wood*, *Aloes Wood*, &c. Of the second, *Frankincense*, *Benjamin*, *Storax*, *Bdellium*, *Labdanum*, *Pitch*, *Sagapenum*, *Myrrh*, &c. Of the third Class, *Sulphur* and *Nitre*, more of which hereafter.

BUT further, that all the Means of propagating the Plague may be removed, it is very wisely ordered by the Magistracy,[211] to kill all Dogs, Cats, and other domestick Brutes, lest these Creatures in their Passage from one Place to another should carry along with them the pestilential Infection.

YET although both the Makers and Executors of the Laws were very diligent in their Duty during the late Sickness, the Contagion notwithstanding spread; when therefore all the Care and Skill of the Magistrate could avail nothing in stopping the common Destroyer, the utmost Application was made to preserve the Individuals under its Visitation: For which Purpose, first of all were removed all Means of rendering our Bodies more subject to take the Infection, and the best Care taken to fortifie the Constitution against its Attacks, and to support it under its Tyranny.

I know not indeed a greater Neglect than in not keeping the Body clean, and keeping at a Distance every Thing superfluous or offensive; and during the pestilential Constitution nothing was worse than Evacuations of all Kinds: But if a *Plethora* required *Phlebotomy*, the Blood should be taken away by a small Orifice, in but[212] little Quantity, and at several Times: A Person loaded with bad Humours, should be discharged of them, if possible, immediately; if they glut the Stomach, and first Passages, they ought to be thrown off by Vomiting, Drinking in the Operation good Quantities of Posset-Drink, in which hath been boiled the Leaves of *Carduus* and *Scordium*; and also the Bowels should be cleansed, to which Purpose the following is useful:

Salis Tart. Ə ij. *F. Solutio in spir. vini opt.* ℥ ij. *tum adde guttæ gambi* Ə iv. *peractâ solutione evaporetur spir. tum adde colocynth. cum urinâ præp.* Ə ij. *scammaii. Sulphurati* Ə j. *Aloes, rosatæ* ʒ ij. *trochisc. de rhabarb. rec.* Ə iv. *gum. ammoniaci in aceto, scil. sobuti* ʒ j. *salis absynthii, cardui ana* Ə j. *ol. carui gutt.* vij. *cum s. q. Syr. de rhamno F. massa, inde pilulæ, min. formentur, Dos. ad* Ə ij. And thus to throw off those Humours which join with and aggravate the pestilential Venom, very much prevents the Want of Antidotes afterwards.

C A R E must be taken that there be no Suppression of Urine; the Non-naturals must be used with great Regularity; the Body must be kept transpirable; the Tone of the *Viscera* strengthened; Fasting avoided; Choice made of a good Diet, such as will yield good Nourishment, make but little Excrement, and be easy of Digestion; to which several Pickles and Sauces are to be recommended; as *Juice of Sorrel, Lemons, Oranges, Pomegranates, Barberries,* &c. and at every Meal Sack is to be allowed, whose Vertues we shall hereafter have Occasion to speak of; and Care should be taken not to be Abroad in the Evening.

A N D to express all in a few Words, all the animal Fluids must be kept in a natural State, in an Equality of Motion, and an equable Degree of Mixture and Fluxility; they must not be put at any inordinate Hurries, nor be too much rarified or exalted; nor must they be suffered to grow vapid and languid, for Want of Depuration, and a Retention of excrementitious Particles. But a proper Regimen is better to be had from other Writers, we therefore hasten to proper Antidotes.

An Antipestilential Electuary of Mayerne.

℞ *Juglandium virid.* lib. ij. *ficuum, prunorum ana* lib. j. *macerentur in aceto, & pulpa trajiciatur, cui adde pulv. subtiliss. rutæ,* lib. [ss.] *viperinæ Virginianæ* ℥ j. [ss.] *rad. contrayerva* ℥ iij. *petasitid. zedoariæ, ana* ℥ ij. [ss.] *sacchari perlati* lib. j. *Syr è succo Kermes* ℥ j. *Syr. calendulæ, caryophyll. ana q. s. ut F. Elect. molle, addendo fol. Auri 40. Dos. ad quantitatem nucis Jugland. maj. mane, & resperi.*

An Electuary for the Poor.

℞ *Conserv. lujulæ, galegæ ana* lib. [ss.] *calendulæ* lib. j. *Theriac. Londin.* ℥ iij. *boli armen. vitriol.* ℥ iv. *cum syr. limonum q. s. conficiatur Elect. Dos. ad* ʒ ij. *vel* iij.

An Antipestilential Confection.

℞ *Radic. scorzon. Hispan. petasitid. contrayerva ana* ℥ ij. *helenii, tormentillæ ana* ℥ [ss.] *angelicæ, chelidoniæ, mai. ana* ℥ j. [ss.] *bacc. Junip. præp.* lib. [ss.] *summit. rutæ* p. j. *sem. cardui, citri ana* ʒ ij. *quibus præp. affunde p. duas aceti sambuc. & tertiam spir. vini opt. infusione peractâ & expressione, liquor igne lento evaporetur ferè ad mellaginem: extracti* lib. j. *adde theriac. Londin.* ℥ ij. [ss.] *boli arm. terræ sigillatæ ana* ʒ j. *flor. sulphuris* ʒ v. *succi Kermes* ℥ ij. *conserv. lujulæ* lib. j. *cum syr. limon. q. s. F. Elect. molle, Dos. ad quantit. nucis myristicæ mai. ter, vel sæpius de die.*

Antipestilential Pills.

℞ *Extract. rad. helenii, angelicæ, contrayerva ana* ℥ j. *adde extract. alb. glycyrrh.* ʒ iij. *flor. sulph. ad quatuor altèm vices sublim.* ʒij. *C. C. philosoph. calcin. sem. citri pulveriz. ana* ʒ j. [ss.] *salis scordii, absynth. ana* Ə ij. *cum s. q. picis liquidæ F. massa pro pilulis, Dos. ad* ʒ[ss.] *vel* Ə ij. *mane, & horâ somni.*

Antipestilential Elixir Proprietatis.

℞ *Croci Angl. opt.* ℥ [ss.] *extrah. tincturam cum aq. ulmariæ, scabiosæ, cardui; vel melissæ s. q. additis spir. sulphuris aliquot guttis ad leviusculam aciditatem: liquor per chartam emporeticam agatur, in colaturâ ad lentum B. calorem dissolve Aloës pellucidæ è vesicâ* ℥ iv. *per sataceum linteum haud ita rarum trajiciatur liquor; deinde F. condensatio ad eundem calorem, acquisitâ pilularum molliusculari consistentia, adde myrrhæ purissimæ* ʒ vij. *flor. vel. magisterii præcipit. Benzoin* ʒ iij. *salis C. C.* ʒ ij. *cum syr. sambuc. q. s. F. massa unde pilulæ formentur, Dos. ad* Ə ij.

Lozenges against the Plague.

℞ *Extract. rad. angelicæ, & contrayervæ* ℥ j. *extr. alb. liquiritiæ* ʒiij. *flor. sulphuris myrrhat. h. e. cum myrrhâ sublim.* ʒ v. *ol. cinnam. gutt.* viij. *saccharum crystallin. ad duplum omnium pondus, cum mucilag. gum. tragacanth. aq. scordii parat. q. s. F. Tabellæ parvæ subling.*

SOME used every Morning to swallow a Clove or two of *Garlick*; and many eat unripe *Walnuts* pickled. The following Draught was of admirable Service:

℞ *Aq. rosar. rubr. camphoratæ* ℥ ij. *aceti opt.* ℥ j. *in quibus dissolve bol. arm. opt.* Ə ij. *adde syr. scabiosæ simpl.* ʒ iij. *M. S. F. haustus.*

SOME old Nurses, as themselves have informed me, for an Antidote gave human Excrements; but for the Efficacy of this Secret, I have nothing to say. Some found Benefit by drinking of Urine; but many who have thought themselves by these Means so well fortified, would venture themselves too inadvertently into Danger, without any necessary Occasion, to the great Hazard of their Lives.

BUT in these precautionary Directions, it is to be particularly advertised, that Astringents of any Kind whatsoever, as *Bole*, *sealed Earth*, *Lemnian Earth*, *Coral*, &c. are not to be given to Maidens, and Women in their monthly Courses, for Fear they should occasion Obstructions, and other bad Disorders: Those Remedies also are as much to be blamed which force this Evacuation by thinning the Blood too much, and irritating the Uterine Vessels: And lastly, in the Preservation as well as the Cure, the Seasons of the Year, Sex, Constitution, Age, &c. are carefully to be attended to.

BUT before I proceed further, Gratitude obliges me to do Justice to the Vertues of *Sack*, as it deservedly is ranked amongst the principal Antidotes, whether it be drank by it self, or impregnated with *Wormwood, Angelica*, &c. for I have never yet met with any Thing so agreeable to the Nerves and Spirits in all my Experience. That which is best is middle-aged, neat, fine, bright, racy, and of a Walnut Flavour; and it is certainly true, that during the late fatal Times, both the infected and the well found vast Benefit from it, unless they who used it too intemperately; many indeed medicated it with various *Alexipharmick Simples*.

IT remains that we now say somewhat concerning the Use of *Tobacco*, whose Vertues for this Purpose are extreamly cried up by *Diemebrooeck*, and some others; but whether we regard the narcotick Quality of this *American* Henbane; or the poisonous Oil which exhales from it in Smoking; or that prodigious Discharge of Spittle which it occasions, and which Nature wants for many other important Occasions; or, lastly, the Exercise it gives to the Lungs in drawing it; besides the Aptitude of the pestilential Poison to be taken down along with it, and the Irksomeness of its Scent; I must confess my self at Uncertainties about it; though as to my self, I am its professed Enemy, and was accustomed to supply its Place as an Antidote with *Sack*.

WE now then come to external Remedies, amongst which *Amulets*, and Characters, demand the first Notice: It must indeed be granted, that it is no new Custom or Contrivance to hang these Charms, made various Ways, about many Parts of the Body, but what Vertues these Things have, is worth some Enquiry.

IT hath obtained with many, that Nature, or the Soul of the World, hath impressed upon some certain Bodies a very diffusive magnetick Vertue; whereupon some *Adepts* have ascribed to many of these Bodies a Faculty of expelling Poisons. Others conceit, that both artificial and natural Poisons do, by a certain Sympathy, when outwardly applied, draw away every Thing that is detrimental to the Constitution; after the Manner as *Amber* attracks Straws, and (as they report of the *Snake-stone*) imbibe its Venom: Some others again contrive *Amulets* of Spices, to invigorate Nature, and support her against the Enemy.

I think it proper to give my Opinion of this Matter; with Submission therefore to these great Men, I cannot easily come into a Belief of any Advantages to be had from this Practice; for most of the Efforts ascribed to them, is rather from the Power of Imagination, or owing to some manifest Property. Furthermore, it hath religiously obtained amongst many People, that Diseases are to be driven away by painting Characters upon the Body; but it is strongly to be suspected, that this Practice hath been altogether owing to *Jugglers*, and

Persons addicted to infernal Arts; for what medicinal Virtue can there be in a Figure? It seems to me, that because the *Sacred Mysteries* of our *Art* were anciently described by *Hieroglyphicks*, the Populace, who were ignorant of their Significations, mistook them for Charms against a *Plague*, and other grievous Diseases, and they propagated their Delusion down to Posterity.

THERE are innumerable Preparations of these Charms or *Amulets* to be met with in the Writings of several Physicians; but I shall take it to have sufficiently discharged my Duty here, to mention those only which were used by our own Country People; the principal of which was a *Walnut* filled with *Mercury*; for it is certain that many did promise to themselves Security from the Dignity of this Metal, which to them seemed to be the Parent of all others; others again expected great Matters from its Volatility, notwithstanding it was thus inclosed, thinking that the natural Heat of the Body would draw such221 Vertues, as would secure them from the Infection. But much the greater Number were supplied with arsenical *Amulets*, from Empiricks and Mountebanks; these were compounded of *Arsenick* alone, with Wax; or had many other Things added thereunto, appropriated to the Disease. One of the chief Forms of this Kind is the following:

℞ *Dictamni cret. pulv.* ℈ vij. *pulv. sinapi* ʒ |ss.| *Benzoin.* ʒ ij. *Arsenici reri* ʒ iij. *ol. cinnam. gutt.* vij. *ceræ opt.* ʒ v. *cum mucilag. gum. tragacanth. aceto rosac. parat. F. pasta, unde placentæ multiformes depsatiæ parentur, ad pondus* ʒ ij. *rel* iij. *cordis regioni admovendæ, linteo serico priùs involutæ.* For it commonly prevailed amongst the Populace, that *Arsenick*, by some magnetick Vertue, draws away all Poison, especially that of a Pestilence. The wearing also of a dried Toad was a mighty Secret with some.

BUT to give my Thoughts concerning the good or bad Effects of these appended Remedies, I do not remember any one who had their Expectations answered thereby; but many confiding too much in them, neglected other more necessary Means of222 Preservation, and brought themselves into great Hazard of their Lives by wearing them; a remarkable Instance of which I met with in an elderly Lawyer, who upon wearing an Arsenical *Amulet* upon his Breast, had a pestilential Carbuncle rise under it, the third Day after which he died. In some others large Vesications appeared, not from any Venom drawn out, but from the Caustick Quality of the Charm it self, and the Communication of its own Poison to the Part: What Madness was it, in such a terrible Calamity, to put the Hazard of Life upon such idle and ridiculous Experiments?

BUT to pass over such Baubles, and proceed to Means that are conformable to Reason, and the Rules of Medicine, *Issues* are not to be forgot; for by these all kinds of Impurities are allowed to flow out along with the pestilential Poison, as through an open and ready Passage; and the more of these little Ulcers are made, the better, although their Largeness may answer as well as more in Number; that is, if they are big enough to hold 4, 6 or 8 Peas together. If any one hath a Mind for two Issues, let one be made in the left Arm, and the other223 in the opposite Leg. And as for the Usefulness of these, I can speak it of my own Experience, that whensoever I was most beset with pestilential Fumes, in the Course of my Business, I could then immediately perceive a shooting Pain in my Issue, and had a great deal of an ill conditioned Matter discharge from it; and this I always looked upon as a sure Warning to have timely recourse to *Alexipharmicks*.

GREAT Service was likewise found in the Preservation against the Pestilence, as well as in its curative Part, by the Application of *Blisters*, and keeping them open a good while.

HAVING thus come to a Conclusion, I think it not amiss to recite the Means which I used to preserve my self from the Infection, during the continual Course of my Business among the Sick.

AS soon as I rose in the Morning early, I took the Quantity of a Nutmeg of the *Antipestilential Electuary*; then after the Dispatch of private Concerns in my Family, I ventured into a large Room, where Crowds of Citizens used to be in waiting for me;224 and there I commonly spent two or three Hours, as in an Hospital, examining the several Conditions and Circumstances of all who came thither; some of which had Ulcers yet uncured, and others to be advised under the first Symptoms of Seizure; all which I endeavoured to dispatch, with all possible Care to their various Exigencies.

A S soon as this Crowd could be discharged, I judged it not proper to go abroad fasting, and therefore got my Breakfast: After which, till Dinner-time, I visited the Sick at their Houses; whereupon, entring their Houses, I immediately had burnt some proper Thing upon Coals, and also kept in my Mouth some Lozenges all the while I was examining them. But they are in a Mistake who report that Physicians used, on such Occasions, very hot Things, as *Myrrh, Zedoary, Angelica, Ginger,* &c. for many, deceived thereby, raised Inflammations upon their Tonsils, and greatly endangered their Lungs.

I further took Care not to go into the Rooms of the Sick when I sweated, or were short-breathed with Walking; and kept my Mind as composed as possible, being sufficiently 225 warned by such, who had grievously suffered by Uneasiness in that Respect. After some Hours Visiting in this Manner, I returned Home. Before Dinner, I always drank a Glass of *Sack*, to warm the Stomach, refresh the Spirits, and dissipate any beginning Lodgment of the Infection. I chose Meats for my Table that yeilded an easie and generous Nourishment, roasted before boiled, and Pickles not only suitable to the Meats, but the Nature of the Distemper; (and indeed in this melancholy Time, the City greatly abounded with Variety of all good Things of that Nature) I seldom likewise rose from Dinner without drinking more Wine. After this, I had always many Persons came for Advice; and as soon as I could dispatch them, I again visited till Eight or Nine at Night, and then concluded the Evening at Home, by drinking to Cheerfulness of my old favourite Liquor, which encouraged Sleep, and an easie Breathing through the Pores all Night. But if in the Day-time I found the least Approaches of the Infection upon me, as by Giddiness, Loathing at Stomach, and Faintness, I immediately had Recourse to a Glass of this Wine, which easily drove these beginning Disorders away by Transpiration.

226

Y E T in the whole Course of the Infection, I found my self Ill but twice; but was soon again cleared of its Approaches by these Means, and the Help of such Antidotes as I kept always by me.

B U T to conclude, it may not be improper to take Notice, that the Citizens much accustomed themselves to certain Compositions for keeping off the Infection, by continual Smelling to them; the chief amongst which was the following.

℞ *Pulv. rad. angelicæ. summit. rorism. & lavendulæ cum floribus ana* ʒ ij. *caryophyll.* ʒ iiij. *labdani puriss. Styracis ana* ʒ iij. *omnibus præp. in commixtione adde ol. nucis mosch. per express.* ʒ j. [ss.] *ol. ligni rhod.* ℈ ij. *camphoræ* ʒ [ss.] *moschi* gr. viij. *cum ceræ opt. p. s. F. massa.* Some likewise would smell to *Galbanum, Oil of Wormwood,* or *Rue,* as also the Oil or Spirit drawn from *Pitch,* and dropped upon Cotton, to be kept in a close Ivory Box. Yet I could not so much approve of these Things, as they were used; because they so much dilated the Pores of the olfactory Organs, as to give more Liberty for the pestilential *Miasmata* to pass in along with them.

227

T H E Purification of Houses was contrived to be done several Ways; but what I most approved of, was in placing a Chafing-dish in the Middle of a Room, or the Entries, or Windows, where proper Things were burnt, and exhaled all round. Quicklime was likewise thrown into the following Decoction.

℞ *Fol. Scordii, Angelicæ ana* M iij. *summit. lauri, rutæ, lavendulæ ana* M j. [ss.] *flor. rosar. pallid. sambuci ana* p. ij. *calami aromat.* ʒ v. *Caryophyll. Contus.* ʒ iij. *F. decoctio in duabus p. aq. font. & tertiâ aceti rosac. vel Sambuc. consimiliter ac lagenæ, à mucore, & setu calcis extinctione mundantur, ita ut liquorem inditum amplius vitient, & corrumpant.* For as soon as the Lime is thrown in, it raises a very penetrating Steam, which seemed very likely to destroy the Efficacy of the pestilential *Miasmata.* For the same Purpose likewise were the following very judiciously contrived.

℞ *Salis petræ* lib. j. *Sulphuris* ℥ iij. *benzoin. Styracis simul liquati. ana* q. s. *ut formentur s. a. Trochisc. deb. exiccandi.*

FINIS.

55

OF THE
Different Causes
OF
PESTILENTIAL DISEASES,
And how they become Contagious.
WITH
REMARKS
Upon the INFECTION now in
FRANCE,

And the most probable Means to prevent its Spreading here.

By JOHN QUINCY, M. D.
LONDON:

Printed for E. *Bell*, at the *Cross Keys* in *Cornhill*; and J. *Osborn*, at the *Oxford-Arms* in *Lombard-street*, 1720.

OF THE

Different Causes

OF

Pestilential Diseases, &c.

THERE is hardly any one Subject more largely treated of by Physical Writers, than that of *Pestilential Diseases*; and the Reason of it I take to be, the Frequency in all Ages and Countries, of Alarms from such dreadful Destroyers; and the uncommon Impressions they are apt to make upon the Minds of those, whose Profession naturally leads them to enquire into their Causes. But in this it has fared as with all the other Branches of that noble Science. The Conjectures and Opinions of Persons have at all Times been too much influenced by the Philosophy in Vogue, insomuch that it is almost an endless as well as an unprofitable Task, to examine into them all: And as such an Enquiry is not consistent with the intended Brevity of these Pages, I shall pass them by, only just taking Notice of the most considerable Opinions, under which, most that has been advanced to any Purpose may be reduced.

ALL Authors upon this Subject, may be reduced under these two Sorts: Such as ascribe them to the immediate Wrath of Heaven, and account them as Punishments inflicted by the immediate Exertion of a Supernatural Power; and such as assign for their Origin some natural Cause.

ALTHOUGH too great a Regard cannot be had to the Author of our Beings, yet Care should likewise be taken, not to ascribe every Calamity to the immediate Exertion of the Almighty Power; for it seems much more worthy of the Divine Being so to order it, that from the Course of second or natural Causes, Punishments shall pursue Offenders, than to imagine the frequent Exertion of his Power in a Way supernatural to inflict such Punishments. But there is a great deal of Reason to suspect, that the Number of this Sect was very much increased by such, as either out of Ignorance in other Causes, or out of an affected Devotion, thought it their Interest to come into this Opinion, and pretend to do greater Cures by certain religious Performances, and their Intercession with Heaven, than was in the Power of Medicine, of which they knew but very little.

OF those that assign some natural Cause, there are several Opinions: Some ascribe them to astral Influences, to malign Conjunctions and Radiations of the Heavenly Bodies.

We find, from the most remote Antiquity, not only *Pestilential Diseases*, but likewise a great many others, ascribed to the same Causes: But all the Reasonings about this Conjecture have been very obscure and perplexed until the present Age, when Sir *Isaac Newton* first taught Men to think justly, and talk intelligibly about the Motions and Influences of those remote Bodies upon our *Atmosphere*. And upon his Theory Dr. *Mead* has since further proceeded to determine their Efficacies upon humane Bodies. By which, as it does appear that they affect us no otherwise than as they occasion the several Variations of the Seasons, and different Constitutions of the Air, the Reader must be left to the Consideration of such Causes.

A N O T H E R Cause is charged upon Steams and Exhalations from putrefying Bodies. There are Abundance of Instances to support this Opinion, that manifestly discover very fatal Effects from such Causes. As Battels are generally fought in Summer-Time, when by the Heat of the Season Things are most disposed to Putrefaction, so it has often been observed, that the Plague has appeared after great Slaughters of Men in Fight, as appears by undoubted Testimony from *Julius Alexandrinus*[1], *Diodorus Siculus*, and a great many others, too tedious to mention. *Ambrose Parrey*[2] gives a Relation of a Plague, that laid waste almost a whole Country, which had its Rise from the Stench of a great many human Carcases that were thrown into one Pit, and left Rotting uncover'd. *Joannes Wolfius*[3], 235 *Forestus*[4], the above-mentioned *Parrey*[5], and *Agricola*[6], all take Notice of Plagues arising from the Stench of putrifying Fish that were thrown dead upon the Shores.

O T H E R Steams of the same Efficacy frequently arise from the Putrefactions of stagnant Waters, and other Bodies, which, in some particular Constitutions of Air, are apt to corrupt and emit very offensive *Effluvia*. Dr. *Mead*[7] relates from *Diogenes Laertius*[8], that *Empedocles* observed a pestilential Disease to afflict the *Salinuntij*, from the Putrefaction of a certain River; to remedy which, he contrived to have the Streams of two other neighbouring Rivers drained into it, which, by their Increase of the Current, with an additional Weight and Pressure of Water, brought the former to its usual Sweetness, and so put a Stop to the Plague.

T O this Purpose Dr. *Plot*[9] observes, the Reasons why *Oxford* is now much more healthful than heretofore, to be the Enlargement of the City, whereby the Inhabitants, who are not proportionably increased, and not so close crowded together; and the Care of the Magistrates in keeping the Streets clear from Filth: For formerly (he says) they used to kill all Manner of Cattle within the Walls, and suffer their Dung and Offals to lie in the Streets. Moreover, about those Times the *Isis* and *Cherwell*, thro' the Carelessness of the Townsmen, being filled with Mud, and the Common-Shores by such Means stopped, did cause the Ascent of Malignant Vapours whenever there happened to be a Flood. But since that, by the Care and at the Charge of *Richard Fox*, Bishop of *Winchester*, in the Year 1517, those Rivers were cleansed, and more Trenches cut for the Water's free Passage, the Town has continued in a very healthful Condition; and in a particular Manner so free from Pestilential Diseases, that the Sickness in 1665, which raged in most Parts of the Kingdom, never visited any Person there, although the Terms were there kept, and the Court and both Houses of Parliament did there reside.

T O this Cause, 'tis very probable, is owing the Frequency of the Plague at *Grand Cairo* in *Egypt*, and in the Island of *Sardinia*, as *Pausanias* and others relate: Although indeed *Prosper Alpinus*[10] charges a great deal of the Cause of that at *Cairo*, upon their continual Commerce with such Nations as are seldom without such infectious Diseases. And for this Reason it is, that we find all those Countries, which most abound with Swamps and Standing-Waters, to be most unhealthful, especially in the hottest Seasons; except, as in several Parts of *Italy*, such Lakes have any Communication with the Sea, or some large Rivers. To this purpose *Piso*[11] frequently observes those Places to be most subject to such Calamities, where there are constant Heat and settled Calms, as such a Temperament of Air most disposes Bodies to Putrefaction and Corruption, as in St. *Thomas Island*, and *Guinea*: And, on the contrary, that notwithstanding the Intenseness of Heat, if the Fluids are but agitated by Winds, Tides, and Currents, there is little Danger of such Diseases; and the less

57

still, the more regular and constant the Seasons are238 upon other Accounts: By which Means it is, that between the *Tropicks*, and even under the *Equator*, it is very healthful.

UNDER this Head it may not be improper to observe, that too scanty and mean a Diet, and Feeding upon unripened and unsound Fruits, are frequently charged with a Share in Mischiefs of this kind.*Josephus*[12] and *Julius Cæsar*[13], amongst Historians; *Forestus*,[14]and several other physical Writers, give Accounts of Plagues from the like Causes. *Galen*[15] is very positive in this Matter; and in one Place[16] accuses his great Master *Hippocrates* with Neglecting too much the Consequence of a bad Diet, and ascribing some Mischiefs arising from thence to a bad Air. And upon this is grounded the common Opinion of a *Plague*'s following a *Famine*; in which Circumstances, the poorer sort, who feed meanest, generally suffer most, as it frequently happens in long Sieges, and Armies ill supplied with Provisions. Thus239 Travellers report, that *Surrat* in the *East-Indies* is seldom or never free from a Plague, which is ascribed to the mean Diet of the Natives, who are *Banians*, and feed on little else than Herbs, Water, Rice, and such like pitiful Fare; for it is observed, that the*Europeans* who trade there, are in no Danger of being infected, because they feed well on Flesh, and drink Wine, which secures them against those malignant Diseases.

A Third Cause is ascribed to Mineral Eruptions and subterraneous Exhalations. *Pestilences* from this Cause are more infrequent than from several others; because such Eruptions hardly ever happen but upon Earthquakes, or Breaking into the Bowels of the Earth by Mines, Pits, Wells, and the like; and then too, in Order to produce a *Pestilence*, it is necessary that whatsoever exhales and mixes with the ambient Air, must be of such a Nature, as to render it unrespirable; or to communicate by it such Particles to the Animal Juices as will pervert their natural Crasis, and disturb their due Secretions; which does not often happen, for there are frequent Shocks of the Earth from intestine Fermentations, which are not followed by any such Mischiefs, as240 they happen only from the Struggle of such Principles, as when they have got Vent, neither of themselves, or by any Thing emitted with them, are of that disagreeable Nature, as to give any Disturbance to the Animal OEconomy.

CAROLUS de la Font,[17] indeed, as well as several others, lays great Stress upon Causes of this kind, and charges *Pestilential Diseases*chiefly to Mineral Exhalations of divers kinds; as *Arsenical, Mercurial,Sulphurous*, &c. which he imagines the ambient Air often to be overcharged with, either from the Heat of the Sun, Earthquakes, or subterraneous Fires. To all this, Persons of different Opinion object, the Infrequency of Plagues in *Calabria, Naples*, and several Parts of *Sicily*, where there are manifestly very great subterraneous Fires, such as occasion violent Earthquakes, and many furious and plentiful Eruptions of metallick and mineral Fumes. A very distinct Relation of which, from his own Knowledge, may be met with from Dr. *Bernard Connor*,[18]who has been very curious in his Enquiries hereinto.

241
BUT however Authors differ upon this Head, several very odd Relations are to be met with in History of malignant and deadly Sicknesses from these Causes. That Story is very strange which is related by *Ammianus Marcellinus*,[19] and taken Notice of by *Cardan*and *Riolanus*, that a most grievous Pestilence broke out in *Seleucia*, which, from thence to *Parthia, Greece*, and *Italy*, spread it self thro' a great part of the World, from the Opening an ancient Vault in the Temple of *Apollo*, and that it raged with so much Fury, as to sweep away a third part of the Inhabitants of those Countries it visited.

IT is needless to trouble the Reader with many Relations of the sudden and strange Effects of some Steams arising from Mines and Pits, which are generally termed by our Colliers *Damps*, because almost every Body has already been acquainted with such Accounts.

DR. *Plot*[20] tells us, That about Twenty Years since, two Persons were employed to dig a Well in the Parish of *North-Leigh* in242*Oxfordshire*, but upon being taken ill, left off the Work: Whereupon it was undertaken by two others of *Woodstock*; who, before they could do any thing considerable in it, sunk down, and died irrecoverably in the Well: Which being perceived by a Miller hard by, and he coming to their Assistance, fell down dead upon them. Another also venturing to do the same, with a Rope tied about him, fell from the Ladder just in the same Manner; and though presently drawn up by the People above, yet he was scarcely recover'd in an Hour or more. And since then, upon a Bucket's falling into a Well in another Part of the Town, a Woman perswaded a strong lusty Man to go down a Ladder to fetch it, who, by that Time he had got half way down, fell from the Ladder into the Well; upon which, the Woman called another of her Neighbours to his Assistance, who, much about the same Place, met with the same Fate, without giving the least Sign of Change; so fatal (says the Doctor) are the Damps of that Place. Dr. *Boot*[21] tells a Story that happened at *Dublin* in *Ireland*, just of the same Nature. And243 in the *Philosophical Transactions*[22], there are the like Relations of Damps in the Coal-Mines belonging to the Lord *Sinclair* in *Scotland*.

THE most surprizing Effect of these subterraneous *Effluvia* that I ever met with, is in a Relation of Dr. *Bernard Connor*, of certain Persons in *Paris* digging deep in a Vault or Cellar, who were so suddenly transfixed by some subtile Vapour, that when a Servant-Maid came down to speak with them, she found them in Postures as if at Work; one with his Pick-Ax advanced, another with his Shovel full of Earth, half lifted up, and a Woman sitting by with her Arm upon her Knee, her Head leaning upon that Hand, with manifest Expectations in her Countenance of what they were in Search after.

THE same Author, from his own Knowledge, gives a very exact Account of a *Grotta* in *Italy*, much talked of, and commonly called *la Grotta de cani*, by this Author, *Crypta* Κυνιχυς; But Dr. *Mead* hath244since, from his own Knowledge also, given a very particular and rational Account of this Place, and the Manner of its killing; to whom therefore the Reader may turn for further Satisfaction.

ANOTHER, and more general Cause than any hitherto mentioned of these Maladies, is some bad and unwholsome Constitution of Air. Such Constitutions may arise from several Causes, which although they affect us in different Manners, yet as they are equally fatal, we call them all *Malignant* or *Pestilential*: In Order therefore to understand the better how we are differently affected by those different Constitutions, it will be proper to consider them somewhat distinctly, under these general Heads, *viz. A dry hot Air, hot and moist, cold and moist, and cold and dry*; to which most Variations of Air may be reduced.

THAT from the several Constitutions of Air, our Bodies are differently affected; and that most Diseases are in some Measure more or less influenced thereby, is quite out of Dispute. *Hippocrates*, in a great many Places declares himself of this Mind: His whole third section of *Aphorisms* is a Proof245 of it; and in several Places[23] he discovers his Opinion, that *Pestilential Diseases* have their Rise from hence. *Galen*, his best Interpreter, understood his το θειον, which some will have to be meant of somewhat Divine, or the immediate Hand of God, to be nothing else but a particular Constitution of Air arising from natural Causes; and that he was of the same Mind himself, is very plain from his own Writings[24].

IT is almost endless, as well as altogether needless, to cite all the Authorities for this Opinion, that might be collected from the most remote Antiquity down to the present Age. We shall therefore proceed to consider the different Constitutions of Air, according to the forementioned Distinction; premising only, that the Terms *Hot*, *Cold*, &c. are used in a twofold Sense, the one is *Absolute*, and the other *Relative*; by the former, *viz. Absolute Heat*, *Cold*, &c. is understood one simple Property of the Air only, as it is different not in Degree, but in Quality from others: By the latter, that is, *Relative Heat*, &c. is meant certain Degrees of those246 Properties: As the same Air may at the same Time be said properly to be both Hot and Cold, or Dry and Moist, as it is compared with another Air, either Hotter or Colder, Dryer, or Moister; for with Regard to a hotter Air, it will be termed cold, when at the same Time if it be compared to a colder Air, it would be accounted hot: And so of the rest. To which Distinction, it is very necessary to have constant Regard to avoid Confusion.

THOSE Countries where the Air is hot and dry for the greatest Part, are related to be healthful, and free from *Pestilential Diseases*, except where there are great Swamps and stagnant Waters, or by any accidental Causes Bodies are exposed there to Putrefaction, the Steams of which render Persons Diseased. In such Countries, for the most Part of the Year, there is but very little Rain, and the Nights are comparatively colder than elsewhere, from the great Dews which then fall. As *Piso*[25] informs us, that the coldest the Nights are in *Brasil*, and the more plentifully the Dews247 fall, the Inhabitants account it most agreeable to their Soil, and conducive to Vegetation; and Physicians reckon it much the most healthful for the Inhabitants.

THE Heat of the Air alone, where it is constant and uniform, does not appear to render Persons born in it, or long accustomed to it, any more unhealthful, than that which is more temperate. *Aristotle*[246] indeed says, a hot and dry *Southerly* Wind will bring a *Pestilence*; but of such we have very few Instances, especially on this Part of the Globe. There is in *Livy*[247] an Account of a *Plague* at *Rome*, from a great Drought; and *Nicephorus*[248] relates such another: But these generally come from some other manifest Causes besides Heat, and in Places not accustomed to a dry Air.

BUT a hot and moist Air is very different. By *Moist*, is meant what arises from sudden or long Rains. This is the Constitution of Air that most Authors charge with being the greatest Instrument in *Pestilential* 248 *Distempers*. *Hippocrates*[249] ascribes a great deal to such an Air, and relates a *Pestilence* that had its Rise from great Heat, joined with *Southerly* Winds and much Rain. *Galen* is of the same Mind, as appears from several of his Writings[250], with many others too tedious to mention. The Truth of this is likewise manifest from the Histories of those Countries, where there are long settled Heats, and afterwards much Rain, as in several Parts of the *East-Indies*, which are known at such Times to be most grievously afflicted with Fevers and Diseases of a very malignant Kind. The same we are informed of from some Places in *Africa*,[251] *viz.* That if Showers fall soon upon the sultry Heats of *July* and *August*, pestilential Distempers certainly ensue. It may be generally observed here too in our own Climate, that the most unhealthful Times are after warm Rains, and the more if the Air is then agitated but little with Winds.

249

FROM a cold and moist Air, we have little complained of, as to their occasioning these Diseases, unless such a Constitution sets in immediately upon a contrary Extream; for all sudden Changes of Weather are more or less unhealthful, as well as in other Respects of living; for which Reason particularly, *Corn. Celsus* advises to be very slow in all Alterations of Moment: And *Sanctorius* frequently inculcates the same in his *Aphorisms*, and tells us[252] how it is hurtful, both to go suddenly out of a hot Air into a cold one, and out of a cold Air into a hot one; and is also very particular[253] in the Inconveniencies of such a Constitution of Air we are now speaking of, setting in after the Heat of Summer. *Hippocrates*[254] does tell us of a *Pestilence* from long continued cold Rains, as likewise does *Fernelius*[255], but such Instances are not common.

THE last Constitution of Air we are to take Notice of, is that which is cold and dry, against which there are a great 250 many very heavy Complaints. *Galen* writes of a most Raging Pestilence about *Aquileia* in *Italy*, that began in the very Middle of Winter, and had its manifest Cause in extream Cold. *Fernelius*[256] asserts the Rise of several Pestilences from the same Causes: As also does *Morellus*[257] observe great Malignities to proceed from some *Northerly* cold Winds. *Titus Livy*[258] likewise mentions a *Pestilential Constitution* arising from intense Cold, but *Physical Histories* abound with such Relations.

OF the strange and sudden Effects of intense Cold and dry Winds, we have very surprizing Accounts from those who have travelled into Countries where they are the most frequent. Dr. *Bernard Connor*[259] beforementioned, relates, That when he was in *Poland*, it was asserted to him by very credible Testimonies, that it frequently happens in *Lithuania*, and some of the *Northern* Tracts of *Muscovy* and *Tartary*; that if sometimes, through the Neglect of the Shepherds, their small Cattle, as *Sheep*, *Goats*, and the 251 like, be left exposed in the Night-time to the *Northerly Winds*, they are frequently found next Morning perfectly stiff and dead, in the same Posture as they are wont to be in at their Stalls and Cribs: And there are divers Accounts of Persons in those Countries, who have been so suddenly transfixed, stiffened, and killed by those *Blasts*, as to have continued on Horseback in the same Posture as when Living, till the Horse, acquainted with the Road, has brought them to their Journey's End: And the above-mentioned Physician[260] tells us, that when he was at *Brussels*, he was informed by a *Spanish* Captain, that of a Party of Horse that was sent out for Booty in a very cold Season, one by Accident lost the rest of the Body; and Riding about some time, before he could find his Way, or any Refreshment, he was so transfixed with the Cold as to be quite killed, but continued on Horseback in the Posture of a Live Person, until his Horse at last happened to find the Way back to his Quarters, whither his Company had before got, and missing him, feared he had fallen into the Enemies Hands; but when they 252 came to congratulate him upon his safe Return, they went so near as to speak to him, and take hold of him, before they perceived him to be dead.

T O Blasts of this kind it undoubtedly is, that Fruit Trees and Plants do so frequently suffer, especially after a warm early Spring, after the vegetable Juices have began to rise and shoot into Buds and Leaves. Instances of this Nature we frequently find in our own Countrey; and I have had Opportunity to observe, more than once, that upon such *Blasts*, the Trees have, on that side towards the Wind, been in one Night's Time quite changed in the Colour of the Leaves; and some, of the most tender sort, almost stripped bare, their Leaves falling off dry, as in *Autumn.*

B U T there is something yet further, besides particular Constitutions of Air, that is taken Notice of by Physicians, as a general Cause of Maladies of this kind; and that is what is commonly called *Contagion* or *Infection*; by this Term *Contagion*, is understood a Disease arising from the Contact of such Bodies or Particles as have in them a Power of Altering the due Crasis of a healthful[253] Person, and inducing still one common Disease; these Particles are generally called by Physical Writers μιασματα, *Contagiosa*, or *Contagij Seminia*; and the Difference of Pestilences arising from these Causes seems much to differ from what have been hitherto taken Notice of, as the former cannot be shunned but by quite leaving the diseased Climate, or by such a Strength, or Turn of Constitution, as resists, or yeilds not to the general Disorder; whereas in this last Case, a Person seems to be equally safe in any Air that is not impregnated with these contagious *Effluvia*, and the greatest Danger arises from the Nearness to diseased Persons, or whatsoever else is capable of harbouring those mischievous and secret Messengers, as the Poet[141] takes Notice.

*Quo proprior quisq; est, servitq; fidelius agro*In partem *Lethi citius venit.*——

T H E Histories of Physick abound with Relations of Pestilences from no other Cause than what arises from the Importation of the Disease, if it may be so termed, from[254] distant Countries; and sometimes not by Persons themselves distempered, but by the Conveyance of these *Pestilential Miasmas* in their Cloaths or Wares imported in the Way of Trade. *Fracastorius*,[142] an eminent *Italian* Physician, tells us, That in the Year Fifteen Hundred and Eleven, when the *Germans* were in Possession of *Verona*, there arose a deadly Disease amongst the Soldiers from the Wearing only a Coat purchased for a small Value; for it was observed, that every Owner of it soon sickened and died; until, at last, the Cause was so manifestly from some Infection in the Coat, that it was ordered to be burned. Ten Thousand Persons, he says, were computed to fall by this Plague before it ceased.

F R O M the same Cause, that is, infected Garments, and Merchandize, *Mercurialis* takes Notice of a Plague in his Time at *Venice*; and *Appianus Alexandrinus*[143] assures us, that the *Celtæ*, after a Conquest over the *Illyrici*, and in Possession of their Plunder, were infected with a grievous Plague, which the *Illyrici* then laboured under. *Thycidides*[255] also, in his Relation of the Plague at *Athens*, intimates, That it was brought from some Part of *Ethiopia* by the like Means. And *Prosper Alpinus*[144], before mentioned, seems to lay the greatest Stress for the Frequency of the Plague at *Grand Cairo*, to the Traffick with those Countries as are hardly ever free from *Pestilential Diseases*. A great many Physicians have charged the Plague in Sixteen hundred and sixty three at *Amsterdam*, to the Infection of some *Pestilential Miasm*, which were transported from *Smyrna* and *Algiers*, then much infected with such Diseases, with some Merchandize; by which Means likewise it was conjectured soon afterwards to reach *London*, and several other Parts of *England*, as it appears from the preceding Account of Dr. *Hodges*. To this Purpose I remember to have read a strange Story, somewhere in *Baker*'s Chronicle, of a great Rot amongst Sheep, which was not quite rooted out until about Fourteen Years Time, that was brought into *England* by a Sheep bought for its uncommon Largeness, in a Country then infected with the same Distemper: And upon this Account it is that the Prudence[256] of those Nations and States are to be justified, who enjoin all Persons and Merchandize from infected Countries, to stay a certain Time upon their Coasts and Borders before they are suffered to intermix with a healthful People; having by such Instances as here mentioned been justly alarmed at the Incroachment of such dreadful Destroyers.

THESE Historical Fragments are put together, in Order to apprize those Readers who have not been very conversant with Things of this Kind, with the various Ways by which the most dangerous Diseases, and even sudden Death, may be introduced into our Constitutions, by the Agency of very minute and unheeded Causes; and likewise the better to support the Distinction necessary to be made between *Epidemic* Diseases, and a *Contagion*; as well as to illustrate the Manner whereby the latter subsists, spreads, and proves fatal, when the Causes producing the former are absent.

Epidemic Diseases of all Kinds and Degrees of Exacerbation, have their Rise from some common Cause, that affects all within its Extent more or less, in Proportion to the particular Fitness of different Constitutions[257] to be affected by it: And by the *Bellinian* Doctrine we are taught, how all those Changes are made in the Blood, when thrown into a Fever by these Causes, even from the most simple *Ephemera*, to the most complicated and malignant Cases whatsoever; to which therefore the Reader must be referred, for a clear Understanding of such Matters; it being sufficient to our Purpose here to observe, that he demonstrates all Fevers to be attended with some Fault in the Blood's Motion, Quantity, or Quality, or in some or all of them together; and that its chief Fault in Quality, (which is most to the present Case) consists in an unequable Fluidity, some Parts of it being rendered thinner, and others thicker at the same Time, than in a natural State; not unlike what happens to all coagulated Liquors.

FROM this Condition of Blood, this great and wonderful Man goes on to shew, through the whole Course of his Propositions, that the coagulated Part, which he commonly distinguishes by the Name of *Lentor*, does accumulate in the capillary Vessels until their Endeavours of Restitution, as in all Elastick Bodies, are greater[258] than the protruding Force, when by the Arteries Re-action upon it, the *Lentor* is shook, dislodged, and washed away into the Veins, and ordinary Course of Circulation, there continuing its Progress till it is either fitted for some Secretion and Evacuation, or again lodged in the Capillaries, to bring on a new Paroxysm.

THIS unequable Fluxility of the Blood arises from two general Causes, either from such Means as diminish its Motion, or from the Mixture of such Particles, as cannot only of themselves be reduced by the digestive Powers into homogeneous Dispositions therewith; or as have a Faculty to put in Fusion some Parts of the Mass, and leave the other thicker than before; these are particularly enumerated, and their Ways of Operation distinctly demonstrated by *Bellini*.

CONFORMABLE to this Change in the Blood, which is the common Promptuary of all the other animal Fluids, every Thing separated from it hath some correspondent Affections; and the nervous Fluid in particular, which is separated from a Mass so unequally fluid, cannot but in it[259]self have some Parts too fine, and others too gross, besides the Inequalities in the Times and Quantities of its Separation; from all which the same Author accounts for those Affections, termed nervous, which are the *Concomitants* of Fevers: And in the Prosecution hereof he frequently takes Occasion to speak of this Fluid to be thin, sharp, hot, fiery, dry, *&c.* as the saline and rigid Parts in its Composition are by the Distemper more or less subtilized, or more or less defrauded of its humid Parts by Exhalation.

FURTHERMORE, in this great Disorder of the Constitution, and inordinate Hurry and Colluctation of the Fluids, sometimes the Solids are maintained in their Contractions and Motions, until the Particles either introduced from Abroad, or generated in the Body, which cannot be assimilated into homogeneous Qualities, are thrown out of the Course of Circulation by the natural Discharges, by Transpiration, or by Abcesses; and the animal Fluids restored to their natural State. But when Matters are brought to this pass, it happens that the very Means of saving one Person, may prove the Destruction of many[260] others; because what is thus critically thrown off by one, hath a Faculty of exciting the like Disorders in the Fluids of another, when it is insinuated into them; as a very small Quantity of some fermenting Substances will communicate its Efficacies a very great Way, and put very great Parcels of Fluid into the like Agitation. And this is the Way by which a malignant Fever comes to be infectious, and a *Pestilence* changes into a *Contagion*; as *Bellini* more largely explains it in his XXVIII*th Proposition* of Fevers; from the whole of which it is manifest, as Dr. *Mead* hath expressed it in his fifth *Essay of Poisons*, that *the Effects of the* one *are the Cause and Beginning of the* other.

TO bring then this nearer to the Matter under Examination, the Plague which is described in the foregoing Pages, was strictly and properly a *Contagion*, and by all Accounts of the best Authority, That which hath made such vast Devastations in some Parts of *France*, and now continues to rage amongst them, to the great Terror of their Neighbours, is also of the same Kind; and was brought to them in Merchandize, and by a Ship's Crew, who were sick of a pestilential[261]Disease all their Voyage Home from some Parts of *Turkey*; in neither of these there being any Manner of Fault chargeable upon the Air, or to any other Causes before enumerated in producing a *Pestilence*.

THE Symptoms of That now Abroad are reported by the best Physicians amongst them to be *sudden Pains in the Head, great Loathing at Stomach, Reaching to Vomit, Consternation, wild Looks, trembling Voice, Coldness in the extreme Parts, low unequal Pulse, Paleness, Delirium, Convulsions, Carbuncles, Buboes, livid Vesications, purple Spots, and Hemorrhages; the last are certain Forerunners of Death*. All which, more or less, are the constant Attendants of all pestilential Fevers.

BECAUSE then there is such a vast Difference between a *Pestilence* arising from assignable Causes in the Air, &c. and a *Pestilence* from a *Contagion*, as to the preservative Means especially against them; and that what we are now in most Apprehension of, is of the latter Kind; it most concerns us to be well acquainted with the Manner of Infection, as far as we can reason about Agents so extreamly minute and subtle. How all other *Antecedents* to a *Pestilence* exert[262]themselves in their Influences over the animal OEconomy, *Bellini* has brought even to a Demonstration; but as to a *Contagion*, he says little; which therefore, as introductory to some following Remarks, we shall here insert.

'As this Coagulation and Fusion may go on so far as to set at Liberty, and perspire through the Surface of the Body, or with the Breath in Respiration, many noxious Particles, which may be so subtil and active, as to enter the cutaneous Pores of other Persons, or mix with that Air which they draw in Respiration, and when got into the Body, be able to make the same Change in the Blood, both as to its Coagulation and Fusion; hence it comes that such a Fever proves *contagious*, which is an inseparable Requisite to a *pestilential* Fever.

'But this is not only thus brought about; but also the dissolved, and dispersed Particles may longer adhere to some inanimate Bodies than others, as to Woollen and Linen Cloaths, Papers, &c. and these Particles may, by the Steam of a living Body, or by the Means of any other Heat,[263] be put into Motion, so as to breath out of those Lodgments, where they quietly resided, and obtain so much Liberty, and Action on all sides, as will carry them into the cutaneous Pores of any Persons within their Reach, and infect them; and on this Account a *Pestilence* may be brought from very distant Countries, lying a long Time in such Manner concealed, and then suddenly breaking out; with many other Circumstances of like Nature.

'BUT if these subtile and active Particles be of that Nature, that they can penetrate the Pores of other Animals, and occasion a like Coagulation of their Blood, not only Men, but Brutes also, will be seized with a *Pestilence*; but this does not always very necessarily happen; because the Blood of Animals is different from humane Blood, so that although these Particles are supposed to get into it, it does not therefore necessarily follow that they must vitiate it, any more than will *Aqua Regia* dissolve all kinds of Metals; but yet Brutes of all kinds, or some of them only, will be seized equally with Men, when this subtile and active Ferment, which penetrates the Surface, is of that[264] Nature, as will taint the Blood of other Animals with those *pestilential*Requisites.

'AS this kind of Contagion then can easily proceed from an infected Person at a great Distance, as often as the noxious Particles can reach another Person, and give that Degree of Coagulation and Fusion, as is necessary to a *Pestilence*; the more aggravated then will be this Calamity, and more easily spread, when a healthful Person is near to one already infected; and yet much more worse, if it is in Contact with those Parts, which more plentifully, and with a greater *Impetus*, breath out infected Steams, as if the Air arising from the Mouth and Lungs, which must be extreamly hot, or the Perspiration of a Carbuncle when it is greatly inflamed; for in this Case the exhaling Particles will be in their greatest

Activity when nearest the recipient Body, and likewise more dense, that is, more numerous, and consequently of greatest Efficacy.

'BUT it is not every one that is seized with a *Pestilence* from Contagion, by Means of Steams exhaling from any particular Parts of the Body; but only when these Steams, and the Air it self, hath joined with, and interspersed through it Particles of vitiated Faculties; and then this Kind of Fever will easily be communicated, and necessarily ensue, not only on Account of what gets into the Body with the inspired Air, but because also the whole Body is surrounded with such an Infection, wherein the noxious Particles floating about on all Sides, will endeavour to penetrate through the Pores upon the Surface, and get that Way into the Blood; for although the Skin is thicker upon the Surface of the Body, than that Pellicle covering the Vessels in the Lungs, and for that Reason it requires longer Time for such Particles to get that Way into the Blood, and the Habit of the Body, yet it is no Argument that they cannot get that Way at all, and be admitted into the Juices.'

BY this we are able to gather, that when a Fever from some Faults in the *Non-naturals* comes to the highest Degree of Malignity, it makes such a Change in the animal Fluids as renders some Parts of them poisonous, and capable of exciting the like fermentative Motions, wheresoever they come into a proper Subject, without any of those procatarctic Causes as gave Rise to the Fever of the first Person seized.

OF what Nature then this Poison is we may conjecture from the Circumstances of its Production. All animal Bodies do more or less generate a Salt; or rather, in Proportion to the Strength of their digestive Powers, do they more or less subtilize the saline Particles which are taken in with their necessary Nourishment. This is abundantly manifest in the Distillation of many animal Substances, which plentifully yield a volatile Salt. But indeed in the Composition of this, in a natural and healthful State, there is joined a very subtilized Sulphur or Oil; which contempers and softens it into a Fitness for the Purposes of the OEconomy: And under this Modification, it becomes the Principle of Vitality, and the chief Instrument of animal Action; not unlike what this is conceived to be, is the common *Sal volatile oleosum*, or any other Spirits drawn from odorous Bodies.

IT matters not what Names Persons please to distinguish this by, in an humane Body; but that somewhat of this Kind is naturally the Produce of its digestive Powers, in the highest Degree of Comminution or Subtilization they are capable of bringing any Thing to, no one will question; and that those minute Threads or Fibres, of which the whole is a Composition, are animated by it; or, to speak more strictly, owe to it their Elasticity and motive Faculties.

IT is hoped, that no one who hath been accustomed to Reasonings of this Nature, will find any Difficulty in conceiving such a Difference of Principles, so finely blended together, as here suggested of a saline, and an oleous, or humid Substance: And whosoever reads *Bellini*, or any others who have wrote in the same Manner, will find continual Regard had to those two Principles, even in the animal Spirits; for without it there can be no Notion had of what is so frequently mentioned, and which by their Effects we find must be true of them, that they are too dry, hot, active, fiery, and the like; or too humid, vapid, sluggish, viscid, &c. And it is further equally manifest, that in Proportion to the greater or lesser Degrees of Motion in those Fluids, from whence this subtile Composition is generated, and the Concussions of those fine Threads into which it is separated, will it err in one or other of the foregoing Extremes.

IN a Fever therefore, where the animal Fluids are in the highest Degree of Agitation, and from Causes too of a coagulating Nature, it ought to be no Wonder that even this subtile Union should be in some Measure dissolved, and the softer and more humid Parts broke and exhaled, so much as to leave the more rigid and saline ones not only unfit to lubricate those Elastick Threads, wherein they reside, but sharp and pointed enough to stimulate, contract, and harden them into all Loss of Motion.

AS the Destruction likewise of this *Nexus* in so subtile a Fluid leaves the saline Parts capable of injuring even that OEconomy which gave it Existence, so may its Volatility favour its Escape in a great Measure by Transpiration, so as to affect also other Persons within its Reach; and These with all other Particles of like Nature, which, by an Over-Agitation, and fermentative Motion of the animal Fluids, are separated from the softer and lubricating Compositions with which they were naturally joined, and which by their Volatility transpire and float in the Air, we take to be the true *contagious Miasmata*, that convey, propagate, and continue a269 *Pestilence*, after the Cause first raising it ceases.

N O R will this seem strange to any who are accustomed to reflect, how many Substances are changeable into a poisonous Nature, which before were not only inoffensive, but useful to the Purposes of Life. Some Minerals, whose saline Parts in their Production are naturally blended with good Quantities of Sulphur, are harmless, and good*Alterants*; but when by any Means those Principles are separated, the saline Parts become strong *Emeticks* and *Catharticks*, even to the Degree of a Poison. Who does not know that *Antimony* may be taken crude in large Quantities without any manifest Effect, but that the Chymist can take somewhat from it, that in few Grains shall operate beyond the Power of a strong Constitution to bear?

T H O S E Arrows of Death therefore that make such dreadful Slaughter in a *Contagion*, are the animal Salts of infected Persons, set loose from their natural Combinations, and subtilized into the highest Degree of Volatility, by the Agitation and fermentative Motion of a Fever. And the Buboes, Carbuncles, *&c.* in a *Pestilence*, are nothing else but Collections of Particles, or270 Coalescences, formed in such irregular Motions, and thrown out of the Course of Circulation by those necessary Laws whereby every Thing is rejected, that cannot be assimilated into homogeneous and like Properties: The Matter of which Excretions is likewise of so subtile and fermenting a Nature, that if introduced into the Fluids of another well Person, it excites there the same Motion and Disorder.

T H I S change of animal Substances into a Poison, is too common a Truth to want any Attestation to those who have been but indifferently conversant in Natural Enquiries. And it is greatly to our Purpose, that even those Creatures, which are generally deemed poisonous, do require certain Degrees of Heat, and animal Action, to exalt their Juices to so high a Degree of Volatility, as to put on the Properties of a Poison, and act as such upon other living Creatures; insomuch that it is not only a common Observation that these Animals lose their poisonous Nature when remov'd into Climes colder than what is natural to them, but that also they are not so venomous in their own Climates, at the cooler Seasons of the Year, as in the most sultry.

271

B U T the Case of a mad Dog entirely comes up to that of a*Contagion* from a Fever. When the hotter Seasons of the Year throw that Creature into Madness, it is manifestly from a great Increase of Velocity and Motion in the Fluids, which brings on what is equivalent to a *Delirium*, by an additional *Impetus* upon the Brain, and for want of so much Room through the Skin for Transpiration, as in other Animals; the chief Evacuation is by the Glands of the Mouth: That is, in short, the Dog hath a Fever, which breaks the natural Texture of the Juices, disengages and subtilizes the more rigid or saline Parts, and critically discharges them by the most convenient Outlets the Creature is furnished with, changed into such a poisonous Nature, that wheresoever they come to mix with the Juices of others, they excite in them the like inordinate and mischievous Alterations.

T H I S Theory likewise might be further illustrated by many Instances from inanimated Fluids, which are capable of being put into Fermentation by a very small Portion of Matter, and which shall by such an Agitation from new Particles, or *Moleculæ* having Properties of communicating the272 same Effects to another quiescent Fluid; not much unlike what we see in the Communication and Propagation of Fire, which is excited and carried on in proper Subjects from the minutest Beginnings, and increasing also in its own Force as it spreads.

W H E N a Person therefore falls into a Fever from any epidemic, or other more private Cause, and that Fever rises to such a Degree of Malignity as is always supposed in a *Pestilence*, as far as any *Effluvia* do exhale from that Person, so far may he be said to have round him a contagious and poisonous *Atmosphere*; because there transpires from him such Particles as will excite in other Animals of like Constitution, the same fermentative Motions as those to which they owe their own Origin.

ALTHOUGH therefore, in the Beginning of epidemical Diseases, and during the Subsistence of their common Causes, particular Regard is to be had to these Causes, and the Manner whereby they affect the People; yet when it is come to this pass, that the Fever it self is productive of a Poison, or somewhat intirely disagreeable, that communicates the same Impressions upon others,[273] without any Concurrence of the first Cause, then such a Fever is truly a Pestilence by Contagion, and all precautionary Regards ought peculiarly to be suited, to prevent its Infection or Spreading; either by keeping the well Subjects clear from the sick, or destroying the Influence of the poisonous Exhalations, or fortifying the sound against it. But to these Ends, it is necessary to have some tolerable Notion of the Manner how these secret Destroyers are continued, and conveyed to great Distances.

THE most common Manner of conveying and spreading a Contagion, observable in the preceding historical Collections, and which also is the Case of our present Apprehensions from Abroad, is by infected Persons, and Merchandize; it being attested by too many Facts to admit of the least Doubt, that even Packs and Bails of Goods carry the poisonous *Miasmata* about with them; and from the Nature that we here suppose this Poison to be of, nothing is more likely to preserve it than animal Substances, as Hair, Wool, Leather, Skins, &c. because the very Manner of its Production, and the Nature of its Origin, seems to give it a greater Affinity with such Substances than any[274] other, and to dispose it to rest therein until by Warmth, or any other Means of Dislodgement, it is put into Motion, and raised again into the ambient Air.

TO know how these *Effluvia* come to have such fatal Influences over Mankind, and to understand their Progression from the first Seizure, to the End of that Distemper they gave Birth to, requires too many *Precognita* from the Mechanism of the animal OEconomy, and the Agency of such minute Instruments, to be particular about, in the Compass here limited. And a Reader who is duly fitted for such Enquiries, will find the utmost Satisfaction from *Bellini* of *Fevers*, and Dr. *Mead* of *Poisons*; how the Blood, and all the Secretions therefrom, are affected, and changed by such Causes.

WE shall here therefore only suggest some Hints concerning the Suddenness of their Seizure, and their Energy of Operation. And this will not be difficult to conceive by those who are acquainted with that universal Property of Matter, whereby it is more or less determined to draw, and unite again, when separated into Parcels, according to the greater or lesser Affinities of their Figures, Solidities, and Quantities of Motion.[275] As nothing therefore in Nature is supposed to bear a greater Similitude, than in this Case the natural animal Salts do with what hath been subtilized and set on Float in the Air, it can be no Wonder that when the Ambient is sated with the former, they readily join with the former, as soon as they are received into the Body. And this is supported by the Authority even of *Bellini*, who allows, in the Beginning of his XXVIII*th Proposition*, that the *Antecedents* to a pestilential Fever do sometimes vitiate the Spirits immediately in Quality.

AS the ordinary Course therefore of producing Fevers is by disordering the Blood first in Quality, with such Mixtures as coagulate it, that is, as make it unequally fluid, some Parts being thinner, and others thicker than natural; so by these extreamly subtile *Effluvia*, in a *Contagion*, the Spirits are destroyed in their natural Texture, and the more rigid and saline Parts, by a Combination with the venomous *Spicula*, changed into Dispositions destructive of that Constitution they were before destined to preserve. Whosoever then considers what must be the necessary Consequences of such an immediate Depravation and Change in that Fluid, which[276] is an absolute Requisite to all animal Action, will not at all wonder at any of the Affections which are commonly enumerated as the *Concomitants* of a Contagion; and a tolerable Acquaintance with the OEconomy, by the Help especially of the Authors before referred to on *Fevers* and *Poisons*, will enable any one to account severally for their Production.

THIS then being the Case of a *Contagion*, that a Person having a Fever, critically throws off poisonous *Effluvia*, which were generated during such irregular Motions of the animal Fluids, insomuch as to diffuse for some Distance round, what will infect other Persons within their reach; and that so many have got this Infection, that no Part of the Air, for some Tract of the Country together, is free from them; the poisonous *Atmospheres*, if they may be so termed, of the infected, extending and mixing into one universal, common *Contagion*; this, I say, being the Case here under Examination, why any at all survive, must be owing either to the Goodness of their Constitution, or to proper Means to defend against its Infection, or to conquer it when received; which naturally brings us to consider these two important Ends, of *Preservation* and *Cure*.

AS for the *First* of these, the common Experience, of meaner People being mostly carried off, admonishes all to live upon as nutritive and generous a Diet as can be procured; and such Things as not only yeild due Nourishment, but Plenty of Spirits, and what easily perspires. For there are many Things of good Nourishment, that are not easily perspired; such as all light and viscid Substances, as Pork, Fish, and the like, which therefore are very apt to go into Fermentation, and generate Corruption; in short, whatever even the common People have Notions of, as apt to bring Surfeits, ought to be avoided, and such Means of Subsistance complied with, as generate a warm, rich Blood; and in Proportion to the Ways of Living at other Times, should every one, except those who accustom themselves to Riot and Excess, indulge himself at a higher Rate.

ROASTED Meats are by all preferred to boiled, and if Pickles and high Sauces are ever to be encouraged, it is on these Occasions; and *Garlick*, *Shallot*, *Onions*, &c. are extreamly serviceable, and preferable to the hot, dry, spicy Seasonings, because their pungent Volatility seems naturally covered with a Softness, or balsamick Quality, more agreeable to the Nature of animal Spirits. To which Purpose it is very remarkable, that in the Histories of many Pestilences, Notice is frequently taken of the Exemption of *Jews*, and People who deal much in such Fare, from Infection. And it is customary with some experienced Sailors, to lay in great Stores of such Things against their Arrival at infected, and unwholsome Countries.

THERE is also a very strict Regard to be had to the Firmness and Strength of the Solids, which is greatly assisted by moderate Exercises, but carefully avoiding too much, and every Thing that occasions too great an Expence of Spirits at a Time, and particularly by over-Warmth. But to this Purpose I cannot conceive any Thing more serviceable than frequent Immersion in cold Water, so that the Times of staying in are as short as possible, the Good received hereby being chiefly in the first Shudder and Constriction; and it is particularly to be remembered, tho' the preceding Author hath omitted it, that Watermen, and others, whose Occasions imployed them much upon the River, and in the Cold, suffered least in the late Sickness. The Use of *Vinegar*, and other *Acids*, are also of Service for the like Intention.

YET besides the Helps for this End from common Diet, and Way of Living, Assistances may also be had from Medicinal Preservatives, such as those commonly termed *Antidotes*, consisting of spicy volatile Particles, which afford a natural *Pabulum* to the animal Spirits, and by carrying into the whole Habit a fine subtle Oil, the better secure them against those Contagions *Spicula* which are in Readiness to mix with them; and for this Purpose, we are furnished with a most elegant and useful Medicine, since many Authors of Note have wrote on this Subject, which is the *Sal Volatile Oleosum*, if it be well loaded with the essential Oils of Spicy Ingredients; although indeed with some Constitutions more fetid Compositions are very suitable; but they all agree in carrying into the Habit somewhat that both recruits, and guards the Spirits against any foreign Mixture, or from unnatural Separations of their saline and humid Parts. And to the same End, in robust Constitutions, who have been accustomed to fare hard, the Spirit or Oil of Turpentine frequently drank in small Doses might be a great Means to preserve the poorer Sort from Infection.

BECAUSE former Writers on these Occasions have given *Formulæ* of things of this kind, much more prolix and inelegant than the present Practice is accustomed to, it may not perhaps be unacceptable to give two or three Examples more conformable to the latter. But because I judge such general Prescriptions rather of Prejudice than Service, when they come hastily and inadvertently to be required by the common People, I cannot but think it much better to leave such to be ordered and regulated according to particular Persons Constitutions and Exigencies.

AS to those preservative Means which a Government only have the Power to provide, they must likewise be left to those who have that Power, but, with due Submission to such, it is conceived that removing infected Persons is a much easier and safer Care, than shutting them up in great Towns: And it was certainly the greatest Error committed in the late *Plague* here, as our Author above grievously complains, to confine the sick and well together.

IT seems a Point yet in Dispute, whether great Fires at such a Time are of Service or hurtful, which to me is somewhat wonderful, because whosoever considers the Necessity281 for Air in Respiration, and by what Quality it becomes of such real Service to the Preservation of Life, cannot think such Fires proper, because they destroy that very Property in the Air, which is demonstrable by innumerable Experiments. As to the Dissipation indeed of pestilential Vapours, or their Destruction in any Manner, they undoubtedly may do Service, but then that ought to be done at vast Distances only from where People inhabit. And what Fires common Occasions require at such Times, are rather to be made with such Substances as abound with, and yield a nitrous Salt, because that seems to be the chief Support of the vital Property in the Air, and such are our common Coals; for every one knows how much more all Wood-Fires are suffocating, and give a Languor, and Flatness to the Spirits.

PRESERVATIVE Fumigations are largely talked of by all, on these Occasions, and they with good Reason deserve to be practised, because while the Poison is on Float in the Air, it may undoubtedly be entangled so as to lose its Power of acting as such; but then for this Purpose such Things ought to be used as exhale very subtile Sulphurs, as the spicy Drugs and Gums. And on this282 Account I suspect Wood-Fires to be bad, because they raise into the Air a very gross and viscid Humidity, which is not only very unfit to lay hold on, and unite with, the extreamly minute Agents that are to be provided against, but also carry into the Lungs with the Air in Respiration, such Particles, as dispose of themselves to Viscidities, and such Changes in the Blood, as are the Production of the worst Fevers, without any other co-operating Cause; for the Fire only forces out that Moisture, which, while a Tree is in its Growth, naturally perspires from it; and how an Air so impregnated is like to be of Service against a Pestilence, any one may soon be a Judge, who considers those Kinds of Fevers which are most commonly epidemical in wood-land Countries.

SUCH Drugs however as are from a vegetable Production, and abound with subtile, volatile Parts, are of Service to be exhaled into the Air this way, both by their Fitness to join with, and cover those venomous *Spicula* that are on float; and to mix with the Animal Fluids by Respiration and Insinuation into the Pores, whereby they convey, as it were, an *Antidote*, wheresoever the Poison is able to penetrate, and which grosser Vapours can by no means do.

OF this kind are chiefly *Storax*, *Benjamin*, *Frankincense*, and all the Aromatick Roots and Woods; and amongst them all, I cannot think the Smell of *Tar*, *Pitch*, &c. is inferior in any Respects, where its Scent is not particularly offensive. And these Things should be burnt at such Distances of Time from each other, that the Air may be always sensibly impregnated with them.

BUT as some have sad Apprehensions from the Air being still, and as it were stagnant at such Times, and not without good Reason, as it favours the Collection of poisonous *Effluvia*, and aggravates an Infection; for the Prevention of which, it is proposed at certain Intervals to fire off great Guns, and the like: I cannot but imagine, that for this End, it would be much more effectual to let off small Parcels of the common *Pulvis Fulminans*, in such Openings of a large Town, as Squares and Market-Places; for whosoever hath been accustomed to any Experiments with this Composition, must have perceived a much greater Shock given to the Air by its Explosion, than by the largest Pieces of Ordnance; insomuch that if any Objection can lie against the Practice of this in *London*,284 should there be Occasion, it is the crasie Condition of the City Buildings, which perhaps may not well stand its Shocks, were they to be made with good Quantities of it at a time.

THE Matter likewise of this Composition in some Measure bespeaks its Usefulness for these Purposes on other Accounts, besides its *Elastick* Force, because it diffuses into the Air great Quantities of that nitrous Salt, which is known to add much to its Serviceableness in Life: And whosoever considers how much cheaper this is to be procured, and how much easier practised than the firing off Guns, especially in the Middle of great Towns, cannot but be desirous to try it, in Case of such Calamities as are now with too much Reason feared; it may not therefore be unacceptable to give its Composition here.

℞ *Sal. Nitri Partes* iij. *Sal. Tartari* P. ij. *Sulphuris* P. j. *optime misceantur in Mortario, parum tepefacto, & servetur ad usuum vase bene obturato.*

THIS is order'd in a warm Mortar, and to be kept close, because the *Salt of Tartar* is apt to imbibe a Moisture from the Air, which hinders its Explosion. A Drachm or two put in as close a Heap as possible upon an Iron Plate over any Fire, will in a little Time go off with a Report and Concussion beyond that of any Gun whatsoever; so that in a calm Season, and an infected Air, great Services may undoubtedly be had from its frequent Practice.

AS to the curative Part in such a terrible Visitation, it cannot be expected that Rules can be given suitable to every one's Case but by such as attend upon them; and the most that can be in general laid down to this Purpose, may be collected from the preceding Treatise of Dr. *Hodges*. Although as to the Choice of *Alexipharmicks*, they are certainly best that are most subtile, and capable of being carried by the Course of Circulation into the finest Recesses of the Constitution, whereinto it is manifest the extream Subtilty of the pestilential Poison is capable to enter: And amongst all of this Class, I take *Camphire* to be much the more preferable; which therefore I would propose not only to be repeated in proper Doses to an infected Person, till a due *Crisis* is obtained, but also now and then given to those who are well, by way of Prevention. And because some Persons, notwithstanding what has been before said, will be pleased with some general *Formulæ* to these Purposes, the following are offered to be complied with, or varied, at every one's Discretion, who is a Judge of such Matters.

℞ *Conserv. Rutæ, Flor. Rorismar. ana* ℥ j. *Species diambræ sine odoratis* ʒ j. *Balsam. è Mechâ* ʒ [ss.] *pulv. Croci angl.* Ә j. *Syr. Balsam. q. s. ut F. Electuarium, cujus sum. quantitatem N. M. omni mane, & horâ somni superbibendo Haustulum Vini albi Lisbonensis, vel Hispanici, tepefacti.* To the Night Dose of this, may be added sometimes 2 or 3 Grains of *Camphire*, especially if a Person feels any Indisposition that requires a breathing Sweat, some may perhaps like the following better.

℞ *Cons. Rutæ* ℥ j. *Mithrid.* ℥ [ss.] *Pulv. Fol. Scordij* ʒ j. *rad. Contrayerv. Serpentarij* Virgin. *ana* ʒ [ss.] *Sal. volat. Viperar. Croci angl. ana* Ә j. *Syr. Balsam. q. s. ut f. Elect. sumend. eodem modo.*

Or,

℞ *Confect.* Tracastorij *sine Melle, Mithrid. ana* ℥ [ss.] *Boli veri, Terræ* Japon. *ana* ʒ j. *Castor. Salis succin. Croci angl. ana* Ә j. *Confect. Alkerm. sine odoratis q. s. ut F. Electuarium ad usum prædictum, precipue h. somni.*

BESIDES a precautionary Use of these with proper Diluters, and under the Direction of those who are Judges; some Security may possibly be had from odoriferous Substances to smell to, especially at a Time of conversing with the infected; for which Purpose I know of nothing so grateful and efficacious, as the *Volatile Sal Armoniac*, well impregnated with the essential Oils of Aromatick Ingredients, and as it is to be procured dry, to be kept in small Bottles, from a careful Distillation of the common *Sal Volatile Oleosum*. But if in any Cases more fetid Substances are preferable, Compositions may be easily made of such from *Rue, Featherfew, Galbanum, Assa-fœtida*, and the like; for these, with some Persons agree better than more grateful Scents.

FREQUENTLY to dissolve in the Mouth the following *Lozenges*, or something like them, I also imagine may be of Service; especially to those who are conversant in infected Places.

69

R *Boli veri opt.* ℥ j. *Terræ Japon.* ʒ ij. *Coral. rub. Margarit. opt. levigat. Flor. Benz. ana* ʒ j. [ss.] *ol. Cinnam. gut.* xij. *Sacchar. albis.* lib. j. *Mucelag. Gum. Tragacanth. in aq. Rosar. Dam. q. s. form. in Troch. ad usum prædictum.* For those who like it, may be added some *Ambergrease*, enough to give a light Scent of it.

P R E S E R V A T O R Y Evacuations of all kinds are much disputed in these Cases, and not worth our particular Regard in this Place; for thus much is plain to all who are competent Judges in such Matters, that but very few Circumstances can justify them; because every Evacuation, unless that of Perspiration, gives more Liberty for any Thing noxious without, to insinuate into the Pores, as there is made thereby less Resistance to its Admission; not to say any Thing of the Danger in such a Practice, by lessening at the same Time the Quantities of Spirits and Strength, which cannot but be mischievous: And particularly ought all Persons at such Times to avoid too lax a Temper of Body; for which Purpose, these preservatory Means just hinted at, mostly tend to astringe the Bowels, and increase Perspiration.

FINIS.

A Table of the Funerals

IN THE

Several Parishes within the Bills of Mortality of the City of *L O N D O N*, For the Year 1665.

	No. of Funerals	lag.
ST. Albans Woodstreet	200	21
St. Alhallows Barkin	514	30
St. Alhallows Bread-street	35	6
St. Alhallows the Great	455	26
St. Alhallows Honey-lane	10	
St. Alhallows the Less	239	75
St. Alhallows Lombardstreet	90	2
St. Alhallows Staining	185	12
St. Alhallows the Wall	500	56

70

St. Alphage	271	15
St. Andrew Hubbard	71	5
St. Andrew Undershaft	274	89
St. Andrew Wardrobe	476	08
St. Anne Aldersgate	282	97
St. Anne Black-Friers	652	67
St. Antholins	58	5
St. Austins	43	0
St. Bartholomew Exchange	73	1
St. Bennet Finch	47	2
St. Bennet Grace-church	57	1
St. Bennet Pauls Wharf	355	72
St. Bennet Sherehog	11	
St. Botolph Billinsgate	83	0
Christ Church	653	67
St. Christophers	60	7
St. Clements Eastcheap	38	0
St. Dionys Back-church	78	7
St. Dunstans in the East	265	50

St. Edmunds Lombardstreet	70	6
St. Ethelborough	195	06
St. Faiths	104	0
St. Fosters	144	05
St. Gabriel Fenchurch	69	9
St. George Botolph-lane	41	7
St. Gregories by Pauls	376	32
St. Helens	108	5
St. James Dukes-place	262	90
St. James Garlickhith	189	18
St. John Baptist Walbrook	138	3
St. John Evangelist	9	
St. John Zachary	85	4
St. Katherine Coleman-street	299	13
St. Katherine Cree-church	335	01
St. Lawrence Jewry	94	8
St. Lawrence Pountney	214	40
St. Leonard Eastcheap	42	7
St. Leonard Foster-lane	335	55
St. Magnus	1	

	03	0
St. Margaret Lothbury	100	6
St. Margaret Moses	38	5
St. Margaret New Fishstreet	114	6
St. Margaret Pattons	49	4
St. Mary Abchurch	99	4
St. Mary Aldermanbury	181	09
St. Mary Aldermary	105	5
St. Mary-le-Bow	64	6
St. Mary Bothaw	55	0
St. Mary Colechurch	17	
St. Mary Hill	94	4
St. Mary Mounthaw	56	7
St. Mary Somerset	342	62
St. Mary Stainings	4/	/
St. Mary Woolchurch	65	3
St. Mary Woolnoth	75	8
St. Martins Ironmonger-lane	21	1
St. Martins Ludgate	196	28
St. Martins Orgars	1	

	10	1
St. Martins Outwich	60	4
St. Martins Vintrey	417	49
St. Matthew Friday-street	24	
St. Maudlins Milk-street	44	2
St. Maudlins Old Fish-street	176	21
St. Michael Bassishaw	253	64
St. Michael Cornhil	104	2
St. Michael Crooked-lane	179	33
St. Michael Queenhith	203	22
St. Michael Quern	44	8
St. Michael Royal	152	16
St. Michael Woodstreet	122	2
St. Mildred Bread-street	59	6
St. Mildred Poultrey	68	6
St. Nicholas Acons	46	8
St. Nicholas Coleabby	125	1
St. Nicholas Olaves	90	2
St. Olaves Hart-street	237	60
St. Olaves Jewry	5	

	4	2
St. Olaves Silver-street	250	32
St. Pancras Soper-lane	30	5
St. Olaves Jewry	54	2
St. Olaves Silver-street	250	32
St. Pancras Soper-lane	30	5
St. Peters Cheap	61	5
St. Peters Cornhil	136	6
St. Peters Pauls Wharf	114	6
St. Peters Poor	79	7
St. Stephens Coleman-street	560	91
St. Stephens Walbrook	34	7
St. Swithins	93	6
St. Thomas Apostle	163	10
Trinity Parish	115	9

In the 97 Parishes within the Walls, Total of the Funerals 15207; Died of the Plague 9887.

St. Andrew Holborn	958	103
St. Bartholomew the Great	93	44
St. Bartholomew the Less	93	39
St. Bridget		

	111	427
Bridewel Precinct	30	79
St. Botolph Aldersgate	97	55
St. Botolph Aldgate	926	051
St. Botolph Bishopsgate	464	500
St. Dunstans in the West	58	65
St. George Southwark	613	260
St. Giles Cripplegate	069	838
St. Olaves Southwark	793	785
St. Saviours Southwark	235	446
St. Sepulchres	509	746
St. Thomas Southwark	75	71
Trinity Minories	68	23
At the Pesthouse	59	56

In the 16 Parishes without the Walls, Total of the Funerals 41351; Died of the Plague 28888.

St. Giles in the Fields	457	216
Hackney Parish	32	32
St. James Clerkenwel	863	377
St. Katherines Tower	56	01
Lambeth Parish		

	98	37
St. Leonards Shoreditch	669	949
St. Magdalens Bermondsey	943	363
St. Mary Newington	272	004
St. Mary Islington	96	93
St. Mary Whitechappel	766	855
Rotherhith Parish	04	10
Stepney Parish	598	583

In the 12 Parishes in the outer Parts, Total of the Funerals 28554; Died of the Plague 21420.

St. Clements Danes	969	319
St. Paul Covent Garden	08	61
St. Martins in the Fields	804	883
St. Mary Savoy	03	98
St. Margarets Westminster	710	742
Whereof at the Pesthouse		56

In the 5 Parishes of the City and Liberties of **Westminster***, Total of the Funerals 12194; Died of the Plague 8403.*

Total of the Funerals — 97306.

Died of the Plague — 68596.

Besides many, of which no Account was given by the Parish-Clerks, and who were privately Buried.

FOOTNOTES:

[1] De Bello Punico.
[2] Lib. 10. Cap. 3.
[3] Tom. 1. memorab. Cent. 10.
[4] In his *Scholium* upon Obs. 9. Lib. 6.

[5] De Peste, Lib. 6.
[6] De Peste, Lib. 1.
[7] Præf. de Imperio Solis ac Lunæ, &c.
[8] Lib. 8. Segon. 70.
[9] Nat. Hist. of *Oxfordshire*, Chap. 2.
[10] De Medicin. *Egypt.* Lib. 1. Cap. 15.
[11] Hist. *India* and *Brasil.*
[12] De Bello *Judaico*, Lib. 7. Cap. 26.
[13] De Bello *Civili*, Lib. 2.
[14] Lib. 6. Obser. 9. and 26.
[15] Lib 1. de differ. Feb. Cap. 3. & de cibis mali & boni succi.
[16] Comment, in Lib. de natalium, text. 4.
[17] Dissert. de Peste.
[18] De montis Vesuvii Incendio.
[19] Hist. 73.
[20] Nat. Hist. of *Oxfordshire*, Chap. 3. Par. 31.
[21] Nat. Hist. Cap. 18. Sect. 4.
[22] No. 3.
[23] *Vid.* Epidem. *and* de Aere, Aquis & Locis.
[24] *Vid.* Comment. in Epidem. *Hippocrates.*
[25] Hist. *Ind. & Brasil.*
[26] Probl. 1.
[27] Lib. 1. Decad. 4.
[28] Lib. 15. Cap. 10.
[29] Epidem. Lib. 2 & 3. de Aere Aquis & Locis. Aph. 11. Sect. 3.
[30] Comment. in Epidem. Lib. 3. de differ. Febr. Cap. 4. de Temperam Lib. 1. Cap. 4.
[31] Vid. *Purchas* Pilgr. Lib. 6. C. 1. as also *Joan. Les* Hist. *Afric.* Lib. 1. Cap. 1.
[32] Medicina Statica. Sect. 2. Aph. 18.
[33] Ibid. Aph. 6, and 29.
[34] Lib. 3. Epidem.
[35] De Abdit. Lib. 2. Cap. 12.
[36] Ibid.
[37] De Febr. purp. Cap. 2.
[38] Lib. 5. decad.
[39] De Antris Lethiferis, Art. 2.
[40] Loco cit.
[41] Ovid. Met. m. lib. 7.
[42] De morbis contag. lib. 2. cap. 7.
[43] De Bello Illyrico.
[44] De Medic. *Egypt.*

Printed in Great Britain
by Amazon